P9-DMZ-718

THE CREDIT DIET

THE CREDIT DIET

How to Shed Unwanted Debt and Achieve Fiscal Fitness

John Fuhrman

John Wiley & Sons, Inc.

Copyright © 2003 by John Fuhrman. All rights reserved.

Published by John Wiley & Sons, Inc., Hoboken, New Jersey.
Published simultaneously in Canada.

No part of this publication may be reproduced, stored in a retrieval system, or transmitted in any form or by any means, electronic, mechanical, photocopying, recording, scanning, or otherwise, except as permitted under Section 107 or 108 of the 1976 United States Copyright Act, without either the prior written permission of the Publisher, or authorization through payment of the appropriate per-copy fee to the Copyright Clearance Center, Inc., 222 Rosewood Drive, Danvers, MA 01923, 978-750-8400, fax 978-750-4470, or on the web at www.copyright.com. Requests to the Publisher for permission should be addressed to the Permissions Department, John Wiley & Sons, Inc., 111 River Street, Hoboken, NJ 07030, 201-748-6011, fax 201-748-6008, e-mail: permcoordinator@wiley.com.

Limit of Liability/Disclaimer of Warranty: While the publisher and author have used their best efforts in preparing this book, they make no representations or warranties with respect to the accuracy or completeness of the contents of this book and specifically disclaim any implied warranties of merchantability or fitness for a particular purpose. No warranty may be created or extended by sales representatives or written sales materials. The advice and strategies contained herein may not be suitable for your situation. You should consult with a professional where appropriate. Neither the publisher nor author shall be liable for any loss of profit or any other commercial damages, including but not limited to special, incidental, consequential, or other damages.

For general information on our other products and services, or technical support, please contact our Customer Care Department within the United States at 800-762-2974, outside the United States at 317-572-3993 or fax 317-572-4002.

Wiley also publishes its books in a variety of electronic formats. Some content that appears in print may not be available in electronic books.

Designations used by companies to distinguish their products are often claimed as trademarks. In all instances where John Wiley & Sons, Inc. is aware of a claim, the product names appear in initial capital or all capital letters. Readers, however, should contact the appropriate companies for more complete information regarding trademarks and registration.

Library of Congress Cataloging-in-Publication Data:
Fuhrman, John.
    The credit diet : how to shed unwanted debt and achieve fiscal
fitness / by John Fuhrman.
        p. cm.
    Includes index.
    ISBN 0-471-25070-8 (pbk. : alk. paper)
    1. Finance, Personal.   2. Debt.   I. Title.
HG179.F76 2003
332.024'02—dc21   2002011153

Printed in the United States of America.
10 9 8 7 6 5 4 3 2 1

To my wife, Helen, for sticking with me on the journey.
And to John and Katie—now we can enjoy the rewards together.

CONTENTS

WHY I WROTE THIS BOOK

PAYING ATTENTION PAYS

A few weeks ago, I was sitting in the airport, returning from a speaking engagement. As I waited in the gate area, I was left with only the airport TV to watch. You know—only one channel, no choices. Well, I thought, I might as well make the best of it. Since I make my living speaking to groups about trends and current market directions, I decided to pay attention to one of the great forecasters of our time—commercials.

As I watched for a period of time, I noticed one type of commercial seemed more prevalent than others. Even though there were different companies, and varied products to deal with the problem, the problem was the focus of the majority of commercials. In a 45-minute period I saw several commercials from companies offering counseling for the problem and still others offering a different way to eliminate it. The problem—debt. The solutions were counseling or consolidating.

One thing became perfectly clear to me. If there were this many companies spending millions on advertising, then it was fairly obvious that debt has come to the forefront of what Americans want to eliminate from their lives. While there are many books that describe the dangers of debt, few really look at it from the angle I believe is most effective for eliminating it. That angle is from one who has been there.

I KNEW I HAD TO DO SOMETHING

The phone calls were coming at a rate of several per day. I got them at work and then later at night and on weekends at home.

How could this happen? We'd had no major catastrophes such as medical emergencies. My wife and I both had good jobs with well above average incomes. When we talked about our situation, neither of us could identify how this could possibly have happened to us.

That, as I soon learned, became the crux of the problem. We were so busy doing our best to live up to our station in life that we never even considered the consequences of our actions. We never looked at the benefits of waiting until we had money to buy something; we just handed over the plastic or signed the papers and looked at monthly payments as a fact of life.

Looking back, we could see that what we had spent on things that we thought we absolutely had to have probably cost us the chance at becoming very well off and possibly millionaires by the time we were in our late thirties or early forties. Now I realize that it's the consequences you don't see that cost you the most. It's not the payment book that's almost full that costs you the most. You begin to see the real picture when you look at the gross income you have to earn, pay taxes on, and then take a net amount from in order to make the payments.

It's like talking to someone who bought a house and took out a mortgage of $100,000. You can look him or her in the eye and tell the person he or she will probably pay about $300,000 over 30 years to finally own the house. That statement won't cause much of a reaction. However, when you reveal that in order to pay $300,000 the person will have to go out and earn nearly $500,000, watch their face tighten up. Ask the person if he or she would be willing to have a half-million dollars pass through his or her hands in order to live in a $100,000 house.

WHAT'S THE SOLUTION?

I tried budgets. They didn't work. Oh sure, they seemed to help in the beginning, but it wasn't long before I began to feel I was doing all this work and leaving myself nothing to show for it.

Consolidation. Been there, done that too. However, that merely created extra cash and large untapped limits on the credit cards that I already had. It only took a few short years to end up right back where I was and then some.

The only thing I was sure of was that I didn't want to live like this any more. I wanted to be able to look at the things I had and realize that I really owned them and didn't share the rights with some bank or credit card company. I wanted to decide what I would spend my money on, rather than scrimp through life on what I had left after everything was paid.

THE NEW CHALLENGE IN AMERICA

While you're living your life and maybe even putting a little aside for your kids' education, there is a challenge that has never existed before in the history of our country. As you prepare to send your kids to school, one or more of your parents may be showing up at your door looking for help. You see, the promises of Social Security, Medicare, and small pensions were not geared for people who are now living longer.

Besides, you in turn will live longer than your parents. Are you financially prepared, or will you be knocking on your children's door in the future? These are some of the costs that can compound themselves when we live today on tomorrow's anticipated income. There are no longer things we can count on in this life. Job security is virtually nonexistent—even if you own the company.

The time to prepare is now. Even if you think it's too late, starting now is far better than giving up. You're about to discover that you are already earning everything you need to eliminate your debt and end up with a secure financial future.

I'm going to shock some of you with some very large numbers. Others will look at this information and question why it takes so long. Relax. The numbers are large to demonstrate the point or the technique and to help you understand that if it works for such large numbers, it'll surely work for you.

You may take a long time to eliminate your debt. You may take less time. My point is, it doesn't matter. Whenever you finish, you win.

INTRODUCTION

GET A GOOD EDUCATION AND A GOOD JOB

My first real job was with the United States Navy. After basic training, I was sent to my first duty station. Once I got settled in, I began to think about what I was going to do for transportation. The first thing that came to mind was to buy a car. I had no money and no idea what a decent car would cost. To find out, I went to the first car dealer I saw after leaving the base.

As I began walking around the car lot, looking at the cars, a friendly chap greeted me and asked if I could use some help. I apologized for taking his time before I was ready to buy a car. Then I explained that I wanted to know how much a good car would cost me so I could begin putting aside the money to buy one. He asked me how old I was and, when I told him I was 18, he let me in on a little secret. "No adult waits to buy a car until they save money," he explained. He also told me he had a vet (armed service veteran) friend who could help me get into a car that day.

I was excited! We then headed toward this man's office. On the way he said that a bank would lend me the money to buy the car because I was 18 and in the Navy. He told me that his so-called vet friend would lend me enough for the down payment. I would then pay him back over the next two years. The car I wanted was $2,400. The salesman told me I needed 25 percent or $600 as a down payment. He then called his friend and told him how much he needed to lend me in order to help me out.

The two of them helped me, all right. When we got to the office, the papers were already typed up. There was a check waiting there, as well. It was made out to me in the amount of $1,000. I explained that I only needed $600, but this "friend" took me aside to caution me about being caught short. He said I'd also need money for insurance and that would come out of the $400 that was left. And to top off this so-called great deal, I was told that I should get a good audio system for my new car. Yes, you probably guessed it—I'd even have enough money out of the $400 to do that, too! It's amazing what some people will do just to get you to borrow more money. And many people, just like me, take this as their *generosity!*

Here's where my downward spiral began. I had not only borrowed money for a car but I'd also be paying for two years for only one year's worth of insurance! To make a long story short, by the time I was discharged from the service in 1976, I owed approximately $4,000—for a car that got traded in on another car, which got traded for a motorcycle that was sold. I owed almost one year's military salary and I had absolutely nothing to show for it. Translated into today's dollars, it would be about $20,000.

What's really amazing is that during the next 20 years, I could actually look back at that fairly typical scenario as the time when I had been in the best financial shape of my life! The problem was, I just kept on creating new debt in an attempt to get relief from my old debt. I kept borrowing larger and larger amounts because I felt I had to have some "extra" money to spend (a very expensive mistake), so I piled new debt on top of the old. I kept buying new cars because I got tired of the old one and kept putting myself deeper in debt!

I had become yet another victim of the Great Consumer Lie. As soon as I could, I established my credit (which is recommended, at least here in the States), and the more payments I made, the more credit they gave me. It got to the point where banks were sending me checks in the mail, telling me all I had to do was cash them and begin making payments. It all sounded like I was being rewarded for being a good little payer. There was a reward all right—but certainly not for me!

You're about to explore both the G.O.O.D. (Get Out Of Debt) principle and how to gain your financial freedom. You'll be taken by the hand and shown what the true consequences and real costs are of being in debt. Once you realize these things and take appropriate action, you'll be on your way to a better life. Let this book serve as your guide to *eliminating your debt and achieving the financial freedom you deserve.*

PROLOGUE

**IF YOU CONTINUE TO DO WHAT YOU'VE ALWAYS DONE,
YOU'LL CONTINUE TO HAVE WHAT YOU'VE ALWAYS HAD**

While it's probably obvious that the subject of this book is re-
lieving yourself of debt, there is an underlying premise that
makes the whole thing possible. For any of the techniques contained here to have any chance of working, you're going to have
to get uncomfortable. The discomfort you feel will be the same
discomfort you've felt many times in your adult life.

It happened when you got a new boss. You felt it in a
new neighborhood. Initially it made you uncomfortable but
when you gave it a chance you often settled in nicely. The "it"
I'm referring to is change. Without it, nothing in your life will
be different.

Much of this book is about making changes in various aspects of your life. You'll be asked to change the very thoughts
that you have about money and debt. You'll be asked to
change the actual ways that you handle every cent you receive. You'll even be asked to consider ways you've never
thought of to make your money do more for you than it's
done in the past.

My part in this process is broken into three key areas. First,
I hope to share enough information with you about the hidden
costs of debt to make you want to change. Then, I'll provide you
with changes in your thoughts about money and finance that

will help you develop changes for your actions concerning money. Then I will share the actual results that you will see, as an incentive to keep you going—especially in the beginning when change is most difficult to deal with.

MANY RELATIONSHIPS ARE STRAINED
OVER MONEY PROBLEMS

Money problems are most often cited as a major cause for challenges in any relationship. I would suggest that it really isn't money but the lack of money due to debt accrued through living beyond one's means. Borrowing your future for a nice life today provides only temporary comfort. When the bills are due, the stress of paying for things you may no longer enjoy becomes magnified.

And, when you decide that it would be best to do something about it, the challenge of change arises. You may have to do without some of the things that created temporary enjoyment in your life. Fortunately, we've created a method to continue to enjoy some of those pleasures with the use of creative financial planning that's really unique.

Everyone knows what money problems are, and most people have experienced them to one degree or another. But some of you may be wondering what I mean by financial freedom.

Financial freedom means you are in a position where your money is working for you rather than you having to work for it. You have enough residual income steadily coming in that you can choose whether or not to work. You get to do what you really *want* to do rather than what you feel you *have* to do just to pay the bills each month. That about sums it up.

"So," you might be thinking, "what makes it worth it to do what I need to do to eliminate debt and become financially free?" There is another powerful motivation, besides the more obvious benefit of having your time be yours to do with as you wish. Becoming financially free is one of the most compassionate, caring things you can do for yourself, your family, and all the other people you associate with. Why?

The stress of financial challenges puts an unnecessary, energy-draining burden on you and your family. And other people you affect can feel your tension too, even if you're doing your best to put on a brave front and be nonchalant about your dilemma and all the challenges it brings. So be kind and loving to yourself and others and decide you've had enough of *the money problem*.

Once you get a handle on what to do to climb out of debt and achieve time and money freedom, you can reach out to others who are also hurting and share with them what you're doing. There are a lot of brave folks out there who need someone to encourage and educate them so they can get free too. Who knows? You may even enjoy helping others so much that you begin doing it more and more! But we'll touch more on that idea later.

The principles and ideas I'll be sharing with you have passed the test of time as the way to get out of debt and build wealth. And they can help you do just that, as you incorporate them into your life. You can get the financial monkey off your back and go on to gain and then increase your wealth. These ideas can help you turn your dreams into reality and bring more peace of mind and happiness into your life.

Money can't buy happiness, but it's the only thing that can do what it does. However, as with anything else, the degree to which you are *grateful* for what you have will largely impact your attitude of happiness or lack of it. For example, money provides a roof over your head, puts food on the table and clothes on your back. It pays college tuition, builds churches, hospitals, libraries, and much more. You can choose to appreciate what you've got, whether it's a lot or a little. However, having gratitude for what you now have doesn't mean you want to stay at that level. It's not putting a stamp of approval on your current financial state. It's just choosing to be positive about what you have rather than negative and miserable. It's a good habit, that's all.

When good people control money, they can do great things with it. But when good people have a cavalier attitude toward money, it slips through their fingers and seems to control them. Being a good person, in and of itself, doesn't guarantee appropriate money management.

HOW ARE PEOPLE DOING FINANCIALLY AT 65?

When money appears to be in control, as many people *perceive* it to be, what follows could be their future. For example, in the United States, many people retire or are forced to retire at age 65. And even though people may be retiring later, their money problems aren't decreasing. According to the Social Security Administration, here's how people are doing financially, in the wealthiest country in the world, 65 years after their birth:

- 36 percent are dead.
- 54 percent are broke.
- 5 percent are still working
- 4 percent have solved their money problems.
- 1 percent are actually considered wealthy and have helped others become wealthy along the way.

Apparently, only 5 percent of the workforce have a healthy concern for their financial future. Another way of looking at this is to say that 90 percent of those who were born 65 years ago in the U.S. are either dead or dead broke! Amazingly, these statistics have very little to do with how much people earn over their lifetimes. However, it has everything to do with *who's* working for *whom*. In essence, *your future will be determined by whether you have money working for you or you're working for it.*

DOES DEBT SEEM TO BE CONTROLLING YOU?

Rest assured that money can't control you—it's just paper and ink! But, when you *have to* earn a certain amount to meet your financial obligations, it sure *seems* that way. I'm not talking about the everyday responsibilities of food, shelter, and clothing. I'm talking about using current dollars to pay for past indulgences. That's right—debt. And if you're in debt, *you* made the decision to put yourself there! The good news is, you can also make the decision to get out of debt.

To help you mentally rise above your financial situation and get a new perspective, we'll spend the next few chapters exploring the challenges debt brings. To best demonstrate various points, I'll use worst-case scenarios. When you read about them, don't just pass over them and say that your situation is better than *that*. The truth is, *if you owe anybody anything, it's hazardous to your wealth*. It's almost like being a slave. You're in servitude and bondage to the lending sources, to a lesser or greater degree—depending on how deeply you're buried in debt. You'll want to climb out of any debt you have, and, in the process, you're taking control of your financial picture rather than letting it control you.

As everyone knows, having money doesn't mean you'll automatically be happy, nor does it mean that you'll become a greedy, angry miser. The amount of money you have is simply a measure of the goods and services you've provided to society. Some contributions are valued more highly in society, or by more people, and thus attract greater remuneration. Your money situation is also a reflection of the degree of responsibility you have taken in handling the monetary rewards you've received so far.

Yes, it's true—getting out of debt and building wealth takes time. This is true when doing anything worthwhile. But fortunately, it's fairly simple, as long as you have a clear path to follow. And be assured that it will be worth whatever you need to do to create it. You'll realize this more and more as you go along.

REPLACE YOUR FINANCIAL FRUSTRATIONS
WITH DREAMS COME TRUE

In addition to your sense of gratitude, your happiness is also affected by how well you balance your priorities and whether you're living your dreams. Once you have wealth, many things will become available to you that will help you fulfill your dreams—without going into debt. You can replace your financial frustrations with a sense of great joy and richness of life that grows inside you as you make your dreams a reality. You can finally experience being fully alive—free of financial burdens and all the negativity they typically bring into people's lives.

In this book you'll also discover some ideas about finding money that you've had all along. You will be given suggestions concerning how to be more aware of where you're losing money and what to do about it, make smart buys, and have some fun saving for the lifestyle you may have thought was an impossible dream.

As St. Francis of Assisi once said, "Start by doing what is necessary, then what is possible, and suddenly you're doing the impossible." Look upon this journey as a great adventure. Picture yourself as an eagle, soaring to new heights, discovering a different world, where peace of mind reigns and laughter fills the air.

TRANSITION YOUR THINKING TO
WHERE YOU WANT TO BE

Start thinking as if you're wealthy. Be one who leads rather than follows, one who wins rather than whines. Sure, it may require new attitudes and habits to do this. However, since you've opened this book and read this far, you're already on your way. Congratulations. You're more determined than 95 percent of the population will ever be.

Getting out of debt and creating wealth really isn't all that difficult. You don't need to be a financial wizard to do so. In fact, many of the world's wealthiest people became so because they needed to work their way out of debt! They just didn't want to stay broke. And you can do it, too! You simply need to make a quality decision and be solidly committed to creating a better life for yourself and your family. *Decide* to get out of any debt you may be in and start building your wealth. As the old Nike ad used to say, "Just do it!"

This book will show you how to get out of debt and build wealth as countless others have done. It requires transitioning your thinking so you can take appropriate action to accomplish your financial goal. It's a clear, simple approach to putting your financial house into the best shape it's ever been in. It's not rocket science, and you don't have to be from the ranks of the privileged few. I'm not a financial wizard, but I've discovered a few basic things along the way that work and have made my life richer.

I'm only interested in helping others grow and become the best they can be so they can live the life they want. It's not a matter of time but simply a matter of steps. Knowing which steps to take will make your journey as short as possible. I believe I've shared those steps in the following pages. *Dump your debt and get free!* Go for it—you'll be glad you did!

PART ONE

YOU'RE NOT ALONE

Recognizing that if you haven't got the money for something, you can't have it—this is a concept that's vanished for many years.

Interview, *The Observer*, 1979

CHAPTER ONE

We All Start Somewhere

The past is a guidepost, not a hitching post.

L. Thomas Holdcroft

DON'T BANK ON IT

When my son reached his 13th birthday, he started thinking about how close he was to getting his driver's license. He started talking about all the different cars he'd like to own. I suggested that now would be a good time to begin his savings program. He would find it much easier to save small amounts over the next few years than to try to come up with enough money all at once.

I had just found out about a new account for kids, 13 and over, at our credit union. This account allowed kids to save small amounts, earn interest, and pay no fees. Since my son was getting an allowance and making money from small jobs around the house, this would be an ideal place for him to start learning about money.

He got excited when I told him there was a way to come up with enough money to have the car he wanted when he was old enough to drive. However, when I told him about my plan, he looked as if I had shot him. He said, "No way will I put any money in any bank." As he said it, I could hear the fear in his voice.

I told him I could not understand why he was afraid. The credit union is a very safe place to put his money. But, no matter how hard I tried, he was determined not to put his money in the bank. His determination made me curious. His answer changed my financial life.

After years of watching his mother and me go through our monthly ritual of writing checks and mailing them out, he was convinced that banks were nothing more than prisons for money. You sent them a check and were never able to get the money out.

When I explained that what we were doing was simply paying our monthly bills, he looked even more confused. He couldn't understand why we were sending money today for something that we bought a long time ago. And you know what, neither could I. It was time we both learned about the difference between money and finance.

COMPOUND INTEREST—
THRILLER OR KILLER

Thomas Edison called it the Eighth Wonder of the World. Yet loans can turn compound interest into a financial ball and chain that can hold you back from the freedom you deserve.

Credit cards compound interest on the average daily balance. This means you are paying interest for every day that you owe the credit card company money. And if you are ever late— even by one day—they tack on a late fee to your balance. A late fee is actually an interest penalty, which means that you end up paying interest on the interest.

That's why doubling payments can pay off debts a lot more than twice as fast. As I will mention repeatedly in this book, by doubling the payments on a 30-year mortgage you would pay it off in a little more than six to seven years.

Here's how: The interest owed on any loan is calculated on the unpaid balance. Another name for that is the principal or the amount you owe. When you send extra money with your payment, that amount is applied right to the principal. None of it goes to interest. Therefore you now have a lower balance owed on which interest can be charged.

EVERYONE HAS THEIR OWN
WAKE-UP CALL

It wasn't long after I had spoken to my son about putting money in the bank that I really saw how bad things were for me. One night, while my wife, Helen, and I were relaxing after dinner, we discussed the pressures of our working lives. In order to provide for our two children, we both worked full-time. My job required that I spend several days each month on the road; that often left just the weekends to do what needed to be done around the house. Helen worked 40 hours a week and did her best to spend time with the kids when I was away. Like many on this treadmill of daily life, we certainly didn't feel as successful as our home and possessions would lead you to believe. Have you ever felt that way?

The first thing we discussed was the possibility of having my wife stay home full-time. After all, I had an income that put me in the top 2 percent of wage earners in America. Surely we'd be able to make it on that. Since one of Helen's many talents is bookkeeping, I asked her to prepare a total of our monthly financial obligations. When I saw what she came up with, I gasped—shocked as if someone had just sucked the breath right out of me. She had added up all our monthly bills and the total floored me. We were in much worse shape than I had imagined. To say the least, this was indeed a wake-up call for us to start paying more attention to our finances.

The fact that I'd had no idea how bad off we were should have been the first alarm signaling trouble. Not knowing exactly where you stand financially is a sure sign you're not on solid ground. Not only weren't we aware of how much we owed, but we were clueless as to what those obligations did to our overall financial picture. Let me put it into perspective.

The average household income in the United States is around $35,000 a year, leaving a net income of about $30,000 after taxes. We were paying substantially more than that just in bills! As sizable as my income was, we wouldn't be able to afford more than hot dogs and beans if my wife left her job. We had gotten ourselves into such a financial corner that both of us had to work, at least for a while. It was like we were sentencing ourselves to continue living the life we hated because of what we'd done in the past. Yet we certainly weren't criminals. We had just thought that being in debt was the way we were supposed to live. Actually, we had given little thought to our debt, and that's why we were stuck where we were.

EVERY LITTLE BIT HELPS

As you examine all your debts, you may become discouraged or intimidated. You may be wondering if there is ever going to be a way out. This book will become your map to financial freedom, but beginning is the single most important step.

There is no hard and fast rule as to how big a step one needs to take. Even a small step in the right direction puts you that much closer to where you want to end up. Most people didn't get into financial problems in one day. The problems evolved from a series of events over a long period of time. Therefore, it will take time to get yourself out from under your debts.

Ninety-five percent of the population will never do anything about this. And, by the time they reach 65, they'll either be dead broke or dead. But all you need to do is send in anything more than a minimum payment to your creditors and you'll achieve what only the top five percent of people ever reach—control of your financial destiny.

Most people who think about their financial situation see only a mountain of insurmountable payments. They often decide to make the best they can out of their lives, which often means continuing on the same path. For some reason, they choose not to examine what is causing that mountain of debt to get larger and simply accept it as a fact of life.

On the other hand, paying extra on any one of your balances moves you closer to eliminating the mountain. If this is the first time you ever make more than a minimum payment, congratulations. You will then be one step closer to living debt-free than you were before.

As long as you continue making only minimum or required payments, the lending institution is in total control. And as long as they call the shots, you can never be financially free. The very moment you make a payment for more than they asked for, the rules change. You are taking control. You are deciding when your debts get paid. You are determining how much interest you pay. And most important, you are setting yourself up for a solid financial future.

Paying more than the minimum changes your position in life. Instead of being buried under piles of debt, you are now on your way to getting on top of your finances. Every extra payment is like another few steps up the mountain. And every few steps will change the view. You will be able to see more and more freedom as you go, which will encourage you to continue when it gets a little tougher. That's certainly better than looking up and seeing nothing but bills over your head.

Throughout the rest of this book, you will be learning specific strategies that will become tools on your journey to climb out of debt. Using the tools as you see fit will keep you in control. As you choose to what degree you'll use each tool, you'll feel the power of gaining control over your financial life.

As you eliminate each of your debts, you will find renewed power. That power is the power of possibilities. You will begin

to be able to look optimistically at the future rather than antici-
pate the same old routine that may have been going on for
years. You can look with certainty toward making positive
changes in your life.

More important, you will set an example for those around
you, perhaps even preventing them from ever creating financial
obstacles in the first place.

THE MOMENT OF SUCCESS

Most people go through life with a strong desire to succeed.
Unfortunately, many don't recognize that they are often at
that point in life where success has already happened. They
don't understand the difference between success and being
successful.

Successful is arrival. Successful is when you achieve all that
you've set out to accomplish. It's a time when you can look back
at the sacrifices and acknowledge that they were worth it, and
that the effort justifies the reward you enjoy.

Success, on the other hand, is much closer. As you go
through this book, many of you will make a decision. Some will
decide that the effort just isn't worth it and continue doing
what they've always done. Those who do that will never stop
chasing success.

A few of you will decide that enough is enough and commit. You will commit to doing whatever it takes to get your financial life back on track. You will practice the ideas in this
book and look down the road at your final destination. You will
say to yourself, "I'm going to do it and that's it—period!" The
moment that happens, you are a success.

Success occurs at the moment of commitment. Stop chasing and start living as you should. As a person and a provider, as
soon as you commit to this journey, you can live knowing that
you're a success. No matter what happens or how long your
journey takes, no one can take success from you. On this journey, the only way to fail is to quit.

Consolidating your debt and applying for home-equity loans are like putting Band-Aids on bullet wounds. You have to stop the bleeding first. . . . You must learn to live within your means.

Newsweek, August 2001

CHAPTER TWO

Where the Trouble Begins

Events, circumstances, etc. have their origins in ourselves. They spring from seeds which we have sown.

Henry David Thoreau

THE HIDDEN COST OF CREDIT—WHEN TO SAY *I CAN'T*

The interest rate is very clear. The terms and dates that payments are due are also easy to understand. Now what happens as the first payment date is approaching? Are you prepared? Is the money already in an account just waiting for the date so you can write out the check? Probably not.

Or does this seem more familiar: "Daddy, my school play (or other event in a child's life) is Thursday night. Will you be there for me?" You think about it and what it would be like to see your child doing his best just for you—and then the reality that you've created steps in.

"I can't. I have to work late this week." You may or may not reveal the reason. But if you're like many others, the reason is to get some "extra" money to pay bills. If that is the case, you may find yourself saying the right thing often at the wrong time: "I can't." It's a simple phrase that often prevents worthwhile things from happening.

What do you really want to prevent? Going to a school play or a ballgame is probably not on your list. But if you find yourself saying that you can't go more often than you can, perhaps you ought to give some thought as to when it might be helpful to use that phrase.

Perhaps it will be the next time you reach for a credit card to get something that would really look good in your house. Maybe you should say it when you're thinking about booking a vacation that you really can't afford.

What if the next time you were considering a nonessential purchase (anything you have to owe in order to get), you asked this question: "Six months from now, when the excitement of what I'm doing today is gone, will I be able to enjoy my life with those I care about, or will I have to work to pay for this?"

If you don't like the answer, perhaps you should look for ways to make the extra money *before* you make the purchase. Then, if it's so important to have this item, you can—and you will feel good about it because you won't have to sacrifice family time to pay for it.

Don't misunderstand. Sacrifice is good as long as those who are doing it are aware and in agreement with the sacrifice. For example, if you sacrificed some of your family time by working extra hours so that your children could attend better schools, that might be a worthwhile endeavor. However, if you asked your family to sacrifice their time with you because of some nonessential thing you "had to have" a few months ago, that may not be a great idea.

THE SIMPLER LIFE

Did you ever desire a simpler life? Perhaps you want to live in the country with a few acres of land, where everyone waves as you go by and what you do for a living isn't as important as the quality of life.

For many people, this scene sounds like a fantasy. To them, even if such a place existed, they could never go there because they *need* to earn what they're earning just to get by.

Perhaps that isn't the lifestyle that you would choose. There's nothing wrong with that, as long as the choice you make is for the right reasons. If you chose to live somewhere else, is it because that would be a dream come true? Or is it because you need to be where you can either earn enough or keep your cost of living low enough to pay the bills from previous spending?

Some people feel trapped at their current job because it pays what they need to make in order to remain afloat. While that's bad enough, what if you were forced to live where you are now and send your kids to the schools they go to for the same reasons? Can you see the possibility for the tension to get out of hand and perhaps even unhealthy?

Where you live or where your kids go to school is not subject to criticism unless the choices were made for you by earlier circumstances in your life. *If you spent your future in your past, your present is seldom a great place to be.*

FASTER (INSTANT GRATIFICATION) COSTS MORE

Debt can control more aspects of your life than you may realize. The negative impact of owing money is hidden and sly. It quietly spreads into everything you do, and eventually what you're able to do is limited by what you owe. Your monthly financial situation becomes the deciding factor. When lack of money rules your life, you are caught in an increasingly tangled web of wealth-robbing experiences—unless and until you take positive action. Even then you need to be careful, because when you begin to recognize that you need to start doing something to resolve your money dilemma, some banker or loan officer is there to offer you *more* debt—disguised as a way out!

Don't misunderstand. I am not accusing your local banker of intentionally doing something that would cause your finances to get worse rather than better. Many of these folks actually believe they're helping you out by loaning you more money.

Why wouldn't they? They've been conditioned, as most people have, that being in debt is okay. When you finish reading this book and succeed in changing your financial picture, perhaps you can share these ideas with them.

Throughout this book, I'll be using examples of the true cost of debt. These costs are hidden under the guise of a so-called low minimum monthly payment. Some of my examples are based on personal experience, while others were discovered through research and observation. Many of them will be worst-case scenarios to prove a point. Their purpose is to give you something you can learn from and apply to your own situation.

One of my first credit cards came from a major department store. I received a nice letter congratulating me on being an upstanding citizen. This was the store's way of seemingly rewarding me, while what it really wanted was to increase the chances that I'd do business there!

Let's suppose you were also rewarded with the same credit card and terms, and you wanted to buy some furniture with a $2,000 price tag. The rate you're charged for allowing the retailer to help you out is around 23 percent interest. No big deal, you say. You're going to pay it off in a few years, anyway. But what if, each month when you received your credit card bill, you sent only the minimum monthly payment of $38? Now let's also assume you never charged another item. How long do you think it would be before you paid it off in full?

As amazing as it sounds, the truth is, it would take you over 30 years to pay it off! And in fact, that $2,000 set of furniture will cost you over $13,680 in payments! For some of you, who figure that it's better to pay a little at a time than all at once, $13,680 may seem reasonable. Others just shrug it off. But very few people understand what instant gratification *really* costs. So, let's take a closer look.

Let's say you decided not to charge any furniture on your credit card. You were willing to buy only one piece at a time as you saved the money from your paychecks. You then began putting what would have been the minimum monthly payment of $38 into a very conservative mutual fund. Since it would have taken 30 years to pay off your couch, you invest the same payments over the same period. Let's say you could earn 10 percent from that fund. Do you believe your investment could be worth over $85,000? What if you got an extra 2 percent and earned 12 percent? Now you'd earn almost $132,000 in 30 years. Suppose you found a fund that allowed you to earn 15 percent? While not common, you'd find it well worth the search because you'd earn $260,000! Now, if you could have been lucky enough to earn 18 percent, that $2,000 set of furniture would have cost you over $536,000! That's what having a $2,000 couch today (instead of waiting for the money) *really* cost you!

Unless you bought an extremely valuable antique piece of furniture, it will cost you a minimum of an *extra* $71,000 plus the $11,680 in interest to sit on your furniture. I've sat on a lot of furniture in my life, but *nothing* is *that* comfortable. That's what I mean by the extra cost of instant gratification—buying something before you have the money.

Has any salesperson ever shared these figures with you when he or she was talking about the easy payment plan? Probably not. If you were thinking of buying some furniture and the salesperson showed these figures to you, would you go ahead and buy it anyway? I hope not. Chances are, the salesperson doesn't even know these figures. It's likely that he or she too has been conditioned to buy now, pay later.

My main objective is to encourage you to think of money differently than most people who pay a steep price for instant gratification. Perhaps you are already aware of how easy it *seems* to pay the minimum monthly payment, and that it's *actually* the most costly, difficult path to take. If so, that's a great start. *Understanding the time value of money and focusing on the long-term consequences of debt is key to your financial future.* Consider this: No matter how short a term—if it takes you more than one payment to purchase anything, the cost is prohibitive. Admit it—*if you can't pay cash for something, you simply can't afford it!* That's the truth. Delay gratification and build your wealth instead.

IF YOU DON'T TRAIN YOURSELF, ADVERTISERS WILL

For those of you who live in the United States and are old enough to remember, new car ads used to be different than the ones we see today. When I bought my first car, the ads focused on the price. This car cost less than that one, and so on. Today, the focus has changed. Virtually every ad predominantly features the monthly payment. You can drive this car for only so much a month. Watch, listen to, or read the ads. They *never* say, "Own it." They let you *drive* it.

Financial freedom has nothing to do with how much you *have*! The *freedom* comes from not being obligated to any financial institution, be it a bank, finance company, mortgage lender, or other creditor. You want the stuff and that's okay. The problem is, you've been conditioned to forget that *you've actually given up your freedom to get the stuff!* The cart's before the horse.

First you need to get your freedom, and then you can own as much stuff as you want—without creating any debt. Since you'll be paying cash, you will certainly be able to buy much more than you could the other way. You'll have the peace of mind of knowing no one can ever repossess any of it! It just depends on the choices you make. Neither happens quickly. No one gets deeper and deeper in debt overnight, and so the freedom isn't going to come instantly either. The question is, "Are you willing to take the necessary small steps every day toward your freedom?"

IS BEING IN DEBT *REALLY* A SERIOUS SITUATION?

The U.S. government is currently operating with a deficit of over 5.5 trillion dollars, and a lot of people are concerned. The buying public has a personal deficit totaling *7.3 trillion dollars*, and too few people are concerned! Let's put that in perspective. If you were to have a baby in the States right now and let it share in this total personal debt, it would owe $25,488. That's $25,488 for every man, woman, and child.

According to the Consumer Credit Federation of America, 60 million U.S. households currently carry an average credit card balance of $8,000. That's a total national credit card debt of nearly *half a trillion!* Just imagine what the annual interest is. At 18 percent, that would amount to a whopping $82 billion.

Another way to look at it is to understand disposable income. Also called "take home pay," this is the money left over after you pay all of your taxes. According to some studies, Americans are spending 87 percent of their disposable income on debt! That means that for every dollar you get in your paycheck, 87 cents is going toward paying for something you bought, ate, or traveled to in the past.

No wonder they say credit is "the American way." But it's not just Americans. People all over the world need to stop this insanity. Today is the time to start! One way to begin is to know where the money goes. We know that 87 percent is going toward debt. However, part of the solution to this problem is to understand what is happening to the other 13 percent.

The first step toward solving or overcoming any obstacle is to recognize there's a problem and understand what's happening. Second, you need to determine exactly where you stand. Third, you need to change your thinking so you can create a new pattern of behavior. And finally, you need to plan what steps you'll take to get out of your current situation. Once you've eliminated your debt, you can build your wealth—but not before. If you adopt the attitude that this process will be a fun challenge, it'll be much easier for you to take the necessary action.

The rest of Part One will illuminate the severity of the challenges created by debt. Part Two will introduce a wealth-building system that creates a strong financial foundation while accelerating the elimination of your debts—*all* of them. In Part Three we'll explore healthy habits and creative ideas to move you more quickly toward your financial goals. Part Four will help you restore fun and balance to your life and live your "impossible dream."

> *The plain truth is this: you cannot count on your employer, the (government), or the economy to provide for you. Your future security is entirely in your hands.*
>
> *Fortune* Magazine

CHAPTER THREE

Would You Still Do It If . . . ?

He (or she) that gets out of debt grows rich.

English Proverb

HOW ARE YOU SUPPOSED TO KNOW?

As you transitioned into adulthood, from being a student to working, you probably received lots of advice from your elders. Perhaps someone told you to establish a credit rating as soon as possible, so you would be able to borrow money when you needed it. As I said earlier, I started to prove my credit worthiness at the tender age of 18. By the end of this book, you'll discover that this action didn't make me a better person! Guess what? When you have your financial house in order, you don't need a credit rating! You'll have something called cash reserves, and you'll love it!

At 18, I was already on my way to becoming—like most people—broke! The fact that 95 percent of the people in the United States never achieve financial freedom has nothing to do with how much they earn. Nor does it matter where they live. It isn't even a question of how smart they are. Most people never get to the point where they are financially secure enough to achieve the quality of life they want. They're more likely to be concerned about whether they can pay all their bills each month. And it's all because of one simple four-letter word—debt!

TOO MUCH OF A GOOD THING?

People can come up with all kinds of excuses in an attempt to justify why they're in debt. Sudden illnesses, major emergencies, and the like are reasonable causes for debt. Yet even these serious challenges can be handled when you're resourceful and accept responsibility. Then why are such expenses so devastating to many people? Simply because they're already up to their ears in debt and they're stretched to the limit. Just to have the peace of mind of knowing you can handle whatever financial challenges you may encounter, may, in and of itself, be incentive enough to get out of debt.

How you were taught when you were growing up often affects your attitude today about different things. Have you ever heard this from your parents or others you respect: "Too much of a good thing is not healthy"? While we could spend pages analyzing the validity of the statement as it stands alone, let's just focus on how it relates to your attitude about money and debt.

First of all, do you agree that you're entitled to the fruits of your labor? Doesn't it make sense to you that the finer things in life should be enjoyed by all who can afford them? Shouldn't you be able to have as much of that as your budget allows? (By *budget*, I mean cash on hand and not the monthly payments you can afford.)

Do you end up in debt to have the lifestyle you think you deserve? Is it possible that going into debt is a form of self-sabotage? Is your own thinking limiting what you can have by allowing you to get it on one condition—by creating debt? While the item may be something that could bring you joy, creating debt to get it is the slowly administered punishment that prevents true enjoyment. Whether you think about it or not, the purchase often comes with a far heavier price tag than what it officially cost. This includes the interest you're charged, perhaps by the same store—the "hidden" cost of instant gratification—not to mention the emotional toll of the anxiety of having to make payments. *You need to break free of the "buy now pay later" attitude. This is one of the first steps toward breaking the chains of debt.*

When you're eating out at a restaurant with friends or family, enjoy the meal totally. Pay cash. Don't create a form of punishment by charging it. The food will taste the same when you eat it, regardless of how you pay. The benefit of paying cash is that when the meal has been long since disposed of by your body, you won't be reminded that you have nothing to show for it when the credit card bill comes in the mail!

HAVE YOU ADDED FUEL TO YOUR OWN FIRE OF DEBT?

If anyone suggests you consolidate your debts, run as fast as you can in the opposite direction. You've seen the ads. "Lower your monthly payments and write out just one check a month." Refinancing all of your debt into one large loan is like putting a bandage on a broken leg. It looks good, but it won't help the bone heal properly. Looks can be deceiving.

You'd simply be piling your financial challenges in a different corner of the room. While the old corner looks nice and neat, when you turn around you'll see that the mountain of challenges is still in the room. All you would have done is to place a mask on the problem without really facing and eliminating the cause. You'd be trying to take the easy way out—a quick fix.

Here's an example. The balance due numbers I'll use are below the U.S. national average by a great deal. The reason is that while many people don't owe as much as the national average, within their own personal circumstances they are in deep financial trouble. Also, minimum payments may vary from what I've listed here. As you see the point I'm making with these numbers, you'll be able to apply the methods to your own situation.

Let's assume the following list is a profile of your debts. (Interest rates and payment schedules are not used since this is only an example.)

Credit card #1—balance $1,000/minimum payment $75.

Credit card #2—balance $500/minimum payment $50.

Auto Loan—balance $8,000/monthly payment $300.

Major Store—balance $500/minimum payment $50.

Total debt balance is $10,000 and the total monthly payments are $475. Now, add to that the cost for everyday items like food, rent or mortgage payments, utilities, and clothing. Remember miscellaneous expenses like insurance, car expenses and such. Added together, that could use up a good portion, or even all, of some folks' monthly take home pay.

Let's say that the $475 each month really puts a strain on the family finances. Then, lo and behold, you see an ad in the newspaper. "Reduce your monthly payments and only have one check to write." You call and hear that you can consolidate your loans into a single payment of only $250 a month. Not only that, the bank can also lend you the extra money so you can put in that aboveground swimming pool you've always wanted in your backyard. This would only cost you $50 more a month—which, the creditor emphasizes, is still less than the $475 you're now paying. If you get a feeling of relief at the thought of the extra $225 you'll have each month, you could be heading for trouble. And if you're even considering borrowing the additional money for the pool, you're heading for even more trouble.

Say you've made the decision to become debt-free and eliminate credit card spending. Let's look at the balances you have left, starting with the smallest. You have two balances of $500 each (credit card #2 and the department store card). In our example, by making the minimum payments, you'd have only 10 payments left, plus interest. Let's say that the interest in both cases would equal two months worth of payments (this again will vary). That means you'd be finished with those in one year.

The other credit card has a balance of $1,000 with a minimum payment of $75 a month. At that rate, including interest, it would take about 16 to 18 months to pay it off. But wait—

you're going to have an extra $100 a month (because you have paid off the two $500 debts) beginning in a year. If you put that money toward your last credit card balance, you'd have it paid it off in approximately 14 months.

That leaves the car loan. An $8,000 balance at $300 a month works out to about 27 months to completion. But in only 14 months, you'll have an additional $175 (because you'll have paid off the other three debts) to put towards this loan. That means in less than two years you could own the car *free and clear* and have $475 to begin saving!

What about the ad for the consolidation loan? It was for a minimum of five years. But, you say, I'd be able to save $225 a month. OK let's compare. By saving $225 per month for five years you'd end up with a principal balance of $13,500 ($225 × 60 months = $13,500). Not bad. However, if you practiced clearing your debts as shown, you'd be free of debt in *two* years. This would allow you to put the $475 a month into savings, which, over the next three years, would give you a principal balance of $17,100 ($475 × 36 months = $17,100). Then you'd be earning interest on top of that. That's $3,600 more plus interest in your pocket!

The biggest difference however, is that by paying off the loans without taking on new debt, you've changed your *mindset. You need to change your mind before you can change your financial life.* You've then eliminated what was holding you back. You're no longer operating on the idea of instant gratification through creating debt. This increases the likelihood that you'll only pay cash and you'll be committed to a savings program.

With debt consolidation, you'd only be masking the symptoms. Furthermore, there's a possibility that you'd be tempted to use this extra $225 as justification for going further into debt to satisfy the need for instant gratification for something else.

You may also be inclined, as the lender hopes you will be, to borrow the additional money for the pool, thus *increasing* rather than *eliminating* your debt! In that case, at some point in the future, you would see an ad. . . . Get the picture? The potential problem is that with enough refinancing of debt, you could end up paying interest on the interest for a meal you ate years ago! Yuk—that leaves a bad taste in my mouth. How about yours?

GO FOR ELIMINATION OF ANNUAL FEES
AND LOWER INTEREST RATES

Instead of getting a consolidation loan, you could look for credit cards that feature no annual fees and lower interest rates than on your current card(s). You could use the money saved toward paying off your debts. People are often under the false perception that annual fees and credit card interest rates are non-negotiable. Often, this is not true.

In fact, a great place to start is to call the bank(s) that issued your credit card(s). Explain that you are willing to shift all your credit card balances and your other banking over to this bank if the bank can waive the annual fee for your account and offer you a lower interest rate than you are now paying. (Then you could close the other accounts to remove the temptation of racking up more credit card debt!)

Making such an inquiry may never have occurred to you. But when you are earnestly striving to eliminate your debt and are committed to your financial future, you explore *all* the options. You take nothing for granted. You ask questions. And, if you are not getting what you want, you ask for a supervisor. You keep doing so until you get what you're looking for, or you keep shopping around, asking other banks for what you want. You never give up the quest!

When you find a bank that'll give you what you want, go ahead and transfer your balance(s). Close the other account(s) immediately and proceed to pay off the balance as quickly as you can. Remember, if your credit card balances are very high, you may need to seek out more banks who'll give you a good deal. Just consider this a temporary inconvenience for a permanent improvement.

BUSINESSES AND BANKS HAVE THEIR OWN AGENDA

You'll need to be aware that businesses and banks will keep encouraging you to purchase things on credit. It's very profitable *for them*—at *your expense*. Their job is to generate business, which is perfectly understandable. Of course banks are going to act like they're doing *you* a favor by granting you easy credit. It's their business to make it look easy to buy what you want *now*. It's easy to buy it all right, but *not so easy* once you realize you've gone deeper into debt. You find yourself juggling your bills each month, trying to avoid bill collectors, and what you've bought is wearing out before you even have it paid for! *You* need to be the one holding your purse strings and building *your* wealth—not theirs. You want to be in the position where you are lending *them* money, right?

Be assured that you can change a financial downfall into a financial windfall. Many others have done it and you can too. And there's no time like the present to do exactly that. As best-selling author George S. Clason says, "Money is plentiful for those who understand the simple laws which govern its acquisition."

Lack of money is the root of all evil.
                                        George Bernard Shaw

CHAPTER FOUR

A Case Study— Jane Debt

To accomplish great things, we must dream as well as act.

Anatole France

AN EXAMPLE TO HELP YOU UNDERSTAND

Before we begin the next part of the book, which fully describes the multiple account principles, it will help you to understand what follows by using a case study with actual numbers. You'll see where the money comes from for each account and the real potential for putting these principles into practice.

It bears repeating that these numbers are averages and not representative of your personal situation. After reviewing this example you may determine that you're in better or worse shape. I caution you against comparing. This is an example to help you better understand the principles you are about to explore in greater detail.

Interest rates, tax consequences, and actual length of loans are not discussed because that information is not important for the purpose of demonstrating what can be done to improve a debt problem. However, those factors may speed up or slow down your own individual progress. Keep in mind, though, that speed should not be the determining factor in deciding to go forward.

Subject: Jane Debt

Salary: $50,000 per year

Auto Loan: Monthly payment $350, balance $16,000

Major Credit Card: Monthly payment $160, balance $8,000

Store Card: Monthly payment $50, balance $3,300

Small Loan: Monthly payment $179, balance $950

Mortgage: Monthly payment $665, balance $100,000

Assumptions: We'll assume that 30 percent of her paycheck is withheld for a variety of taxes. No rates or compounding will be used. Taxes, utilities, and insurance, as well as food and other living expenses, are not calculated.

At a 30 percent tax rate, Jane has a monthly net income of $2,901. The total of her monthly payments is $1,404. That leaves a spendable balance of $1,497 for food, clothing, insurance (car, home, life), utilities, property taxes, and emergencies.

At this point, Jane has nothing in the bank and feels that there is little she can do to start saving.

Since the mortgage is new, she has the full 30 years left. (Later, I will show how you can double your mortgage payments and save a fortune. In Jane's case, she could own her home free and clear in less than seven years.)

Each month, Jane will receive her paycheck of $2,901 and we will track what happens to it using our formula. In order to determine how much will be placed into each of the accounts that follow, I will use the formula found in the tables at the end of the book. This formula is not the only combination that can be used. In fact, any combination will work; however, the time it takes to achieve your individual objectives will be determined by your own debt and how you distribute your funds.

I determined how much to put into each account by first determining the personal debt ratio. You do this by dividing what you pay each month by what you earn. Since Jane's goal is to eliminate debt as quickly as possible and then develop a strong savings strategy, we'll use the same formula. In this example we calculate $1,404 ÷ 2,901 = .48 or 48 percent. We'll round it off to 50 percent.

We will be using 10 percent of Jane's current income in the following example. This will demonstrate how you can change your financial future with as little as 10 percent of what you're currently earning. Later in the book you'll see ways to increase your earnings and thus accelerate your success. But for now it's important to see that this whole process can be attained using only 10 percent of current earnings.

That means that of the 10 percent Jane will use in her accounts (we'll use $290 for that amount), 50 percent will go directly into the Debt Elimination account. The other account percentages are arbitrary and can be made in your order of preference. For our purposes, Jane's accounts will have these percentages to divide her monthly contribution of $290:

Permanent Wealth Account	10% or $29
Totally Fun Account	20% or $58
Future Growth Account	10% or $29
Income Security Account	10% or $29
Debt Elimination Account	50% or $145

Now we can begin.

As you can see by the preceding list, Jane has $290 distributed among five accounts after the first month. Now she will continue meeting her obligations and live on 90 percent of what she earns. This may sound difficult since many of you are convinced that you're not making enough in the first place, and now I'm asking you to do the same with less. However, I'm confident that if you take a look at the results in your own life after 90 days, you'll see more than enough proof that it's worth the effort.

AFTER THE FIRST 90 DAYS

In 90 days Jane's financial picture will look like this:

Permanent Wealth Account	10% or $87
Totally Fun Account	20% or $174
Future Growth Account	10% or $87
Income Security Account	10% or $87
Debt Elimination Account	50% or $435

The fact that she was able to put aside $870 should be enough incentive to keep you interested. However, the real motivation comes into play when she uses each account for what it was intended for. I've rearranged her current debts in the order that they should be eliminated.

Small Loan: Monthly payment $179, balance $950

Store Card: Monthly payment $50, balance $3,300

Major Credit Card: Monthly payment $160, balance $8,000

Auto Loan: Monthly payment $350, balance $16,000

Mortgage: Monthly payment $665, balance $100,000

Since we began, Jane has made three payments on each of these debts, in addition to setting aside money in her accounts. Therefore, all of her balances have been reduced. Some have gone down more than others have, but we will be applying all of the money in her Debt Elimination Account toward the first bill on her new list. This will be the one that will be paid off entirely, first.

Small Loan: Monthly payment $179, balance $575

Store Card: Monthly payment $50, balance $3,275

Major Credit Card: Monthly payment $160, balance $7,950

Auto Loan: Monthly payment $350, balance $15,400

Mortgage: Monthly payment $665, balance $99,750

(*Note:* The balances are decreasing by an amount smaller than the total payment. This is to demonstrate the effects of interest and finance charges on each of the accounts. While not exact calculations, they more than demonstrate the principles.)

Looking at Jane's Debt Elimination Account, you'll find a balance of $435. For this example, we'll be using all of it. (A portion will be left in the account to keep it open. That amount will be determined by your own banking institution.) If we apply the $435 to the first debt on the list, the balance owed would be reduced to $140. The reason for this reduction is because anything you pay over and above the minimum payment is applied totally toward the principal.

To celebrate her newfound financial power, Jane can go to her Totally Fun account and withdraw $174 to spend on anything she would like, and not have to worry about being billed for it in the future. After just 90 days, Jane is able to see the power you get when you take control of your finances. She has the incentive to keep going at least for another 90 days.

THE SECOND 90 DAYS

After the next 90 days, some of Jane's accounts have grown even further. The Permanent Wealth, Future Growth, and Income Security accounts are twice what they were last time. The Totally Fun account is built back up to where it was before she took the money out and had some guilt-free fun. However, look at the Debt Elimination account. I'll explain that one in more detail.

Permanent Wealth Account	10% or $174
Totally Fun Account	20% or $174
Future Growth Account	10% or $174
Income Security Account	10% or $174
Debt Elimination Account	50% or $882

How is it possible that this account grew so much, especially after Jane emptied it to pay down one of her bills? This is
where the power of the multiple account principle really
demonstrates itself. Look back at the balance of Jane's small
loan. Since she attacked that one first and paid all of the money
from the Debt Elimination account toward it, the balance at the
beginning of the second 90 days was only $140. That meant she
would have $39 left over after she made the final monthly pay-
ment (Payment $179 – Balance $140 = $39). In addition to that,
she *continues* to make the monthly $179 payment—into her
Debt Elimination account.

This is very important! With each obligation that gets paid
in full, the payment you had been making continues. The only
difference is that instead of sending it to some bank or department store, you now send it to yourself and deposit it in your
Debt Elimination account.

After just six months on her credit diet, Jane has totally
eliminated one debt, saved $522, and can go out again and
spend $174 on anything she desires. However, since she now
has additional money going into her Debt Elimination account,
things will start to accelerate and get exciting.

NOW THE EXCITEMENT STARTS

The third 90 days will begin to truly demonstrate the power of
finance for Jane. She will really accelerate her debt elimination
from this point forward. As long as she adheres to her own
guidelines, her financial future is beginning to build a solid
foundation. In fact, she only has four bills left. Here are the ap-
proximate balances on each:

Store Card: Monthly payment $50, balance $3,250

Major Credit Card: Monthly payment $160, balance $7,700

Auto Loan: Monthly payment $350, balance $15,100

Mortgage: Monthly payment $665, balance $99,500

Now let's can look at her accounts and see where she stands.

Permanent Wealth Account	10% or $261
Totally Fun Account	20% or $174
Future Growth Account	10% or $261
Income Security Account	10% or $261
Debt Elimination Account	50% or $972

Now Jane sets her sights on the next target, which will be her store credit card account. As she empties her Debt Elimination account, all of that money will be applied to the balance of the targeted account. That means she'll now have a balance of $3,250–$972, or $2,278.

In two more 90-day periods her balance on that store account would be down to approximately $100. Then she would begin attacking her next debt, which would be her major credit card. Her balances would look like this:

Major Credit Card: Monthly payment $160, balance $7,000
Auto Loan: Monthly payment $350, balance $13,600
Mortgage: Monthly payment $665, balance $98,100

Her accounts would now look like this:

Permanent Wealth Account	10% or $435
Totally Fun Account	20% or $174
Future Growth Account	10% or $435
Income Security Account	10% or $435
Debt Elimination Account	50% or $1,022

Taking her Debt Elimination balance and applying it to her major credit card would reduce the balance to $5,978. She would have approximately $1,305 in her accounts and once again would be able to spend $174 on anything she wanted to reward her efforts.

The last part of this example is to take a look at where Jane ends up after just two years on this program. The examples aren't taking into account any increase in earnings, interest earned, or the possibility of lower rates available on her outstanding loans. However, compare her results with where you are now as opposed to where you were two years ago. Can you see the importance of giving this program a real chance in your life?

At the end of two years, Jane's debts would look something like this:

Major Credit Card: Monthly payment $160, balance $4,156

Auto Loan: Monthly payment $350, balance $11,800

Mortgage: Monthly payment $665, balance $97,500

She would also have these balances in her accounts:

Permanent Wealth Account	10% or $609
Totally Fun Account	20% or $174
Future Growth Account	10% or $609
Income Security Account	10% or $609
Debt Elimination Account	50% or $1,122

(This amount was already applied to the major credit card balance).

Considering that no matter what she did with her life, two years were going to pass anyway, I think you'll agree that she made a good choice. More than likely Jane has seen enough proof to go on with the program. Should she do that, here are the projected results.

- At the end of three years, her major credit card would be paid off and an additional $160 would be going into her Debt Elimination Account each month.
- At the end of four years, the car would be paid for with about $1,800 left over to begin attacking the mortgage.
- Beginning with the first 90 days of the fifth year, an additional $10,000 per year would be paid toward her mortgage.

Her other accounts would look like this:

Permanent Wealth Account	10% or $1,218
Totally Fun Account	20% or $174
Future Growth Account	10% or $1,218
Income Security Account	10% or $1,218
Debt Elimination Account	50% or $2,652

The bottom line is, Jane went from having no savings to having over $3,600 in the bank in four short years. That may not seem like much, but she also eliminated $28,250 in debt, and if she continues with the plan she will eliminate the final 20 years of her mortgage, which will save her an additional $159,000 in interest.

The short time that Jane has been on this program has given her something that is even more important than simply eliminating some bills. Even at the two-year point in the program, Jane has options. She has some money in accounts that can cover her in the event of an emergency and has reduced her monthly obligations by nearly $200.

Even though she's continuing to apply that freed-up $2,400 per year toward her other debts, if she were laid off for a period of time or had to take a reduction in pay, she would be in much better shape than if she had continued the way she was originally handling her money.

What would your life be like if you had more options? More important, are you willing to go forward with this program, knowing that it will definitely create those options for you? I hope so.

The secret to success is to do the common things uncommonly well.

John D. Rockefeller, Jr.

CHAPTER FIVE

Thinking Wealthy

If you do the things you need to do when you need to do them, then someday you can do the things you want to do when you want to do them.

Zig Ziglar

FREEDOM MEANS OPTIONS

As I said earlier, the amount of money you earn or have doesn't determine your freedom. That is determined by your ability to have what you need to enjoy the life you want, without settling for less. Freedom means that you have more options.

You can go on vacation and decide when you're coming back *after you get there.* You can enjoy restaurants because of their ambiance and type of cuisine rather than what they charge. (You won't have to look at the right side of the menu first— where the prices are!) You can look forward to receiving your mail rather than dreading the bills, because you're out of debt and have plenty of money to pay household expenses and to buy what you really want.

How much money do you need to be free? Let's say you're currently earning $50,000 a year. If you want to retire early from your job, say in two years, how much income would you *really need* to enjoy your life as much as you would like to? If you were to answer that question right now, you'd probably make a common mistake.

You need more information. Let's say you owe money on your home, on one of your two cars, and on your three (U.S.

national average) credit cards. Your mortgage is $1,000 a month, the car is $325 a month, and the monthly total for the credit cards is $200 (which is an extremely conservative figure). From here on you can use your history to help you shape your future.

If you decided to stop borrowing and just pay the bills when they come, you'd need $50,000 a year to maintain your lifestyle. To retire would require a nest egg of between $500,000 and $1,000,000, earning between 5 percent and 10 percent interest per year. (To keep this simple, I won't be compounding interest, calculating income tax, or considering inflation. All of those factors would change the numbers but not the principle in this example.)

If you don't have that amount in the bank, you'd virtually be forced to keep on working at your job. Working somewhere when you've put yourself in the financial position where you basically don't have a choice affects how you feel about the job. You can begin to feel trapped and forced into situations that normally you'd refuse to be involved with. For example, in a downsizing, you may be unexpectedly transferred to another location that is hundreds of miles from your hometown. If you don't go, you may be forced out. You decide you've got to uproot your family and move to take the new job. Unfortunately, you need this job *because of your bills*.

Let's look at another possibility. Suppose you agreed to work harder than anyone else in your position. The quality of your work becomes second to none. The reason you're willing to do this is because you know it's short-term. You're only going to do it until you're debt-free. Since your mind knows this is only a temporary situation, you handle any challenge that pops up at work much more easily because you know you're moving on.

In the example, you're now paying $1,525 per month in bills. That means $18,300 per year of your salary is going to pay off debt. While the rest of this book deals with the specifics of eliminating that debt and achieving financial freedom, picture yourself unloading your debt right now. Imagine rewarding yourself with many *options* now. Once those debts are gone, feel how your confidence and security are touching the sky. Look at how your dreams are unfolding right in front of you . . .

REAL POSSIBILITIES TO PREPARE FOR

Let's say there are two of you at work with the exact same situation. You took a "life jacket"—you committed yourself to get out of debt and you did it—but your co-worker didn't. The day you paid the last payment, both of you got laid off. Which of you has greater options? One of you *must* find a job that pays $50,000. You, however, can get one that pays anywhere from $31,700 to $50,000. Who has a better chance of finding work?

If you found a job that pays $31,700, it would probably be an easier one. Yet you'd still be able to maintain your current lifestyle because you've eliminated your debt! Without that hanging over your head, you've become a happier, more productive employee. We'll call this Option #1.

If you found a job that pays more than $31,700, you'd have additional money you could put in the bank to *invest*. In fact, if you replaced your job with one that pays the same ($50,000), the $18,300 you *were* paying in bills could go directly into the bank. If you did that, you could have one year's living expenses (you need $31,700 to maintain your lifestyle) saved in less than two years! In essence, for every two years you work, you could take one off without sacrificing anything! We'll call this Option #2.

Imagine working this way for the next few years. Can you see that *early* retirement is a closer possibility than you once thought? Do you realize that if you could earn 10 percent on your investments, you'd need only $317,000 in savings to provide the income you need to retire? That's certainly less than a million and a lot easier to raise when you're saving over $18,000 a year! We'll call this Option #3.

RETHINKING WHAT WEALTH IS

Before you started reading this book, you probably had an idea of what wealth meant to you. Your thoughts may have centered around million-dollar bank accounts" and huge investment portfolios. If so, it's also possible that because of the size of those numbers, you had other thoughts about the impossibility of becoming wealthy yourself. You may have considered being wealthy as a wish that would stay a wish, and that was as close as you'd ever get. Whatever your thoughts have been about wealth has affected where you are financially right now.

Take the million-dollar bank account. Would that make you wealthy? Since we're only in the first part of the book, I'm not going to discuss interest or investment earnings yet. So let's just talk about having a million dollars. How many times have you had the discussion with friends about what you could do with a million dollars? Invariably, someone in the conversation would say, "You could never spend a million dollars." To which some-one else always replied, "Give it to me. I'll spend it!"

Well, let's do it! We'll start small. I want you to picture $500 in your hands. There are no bills to pay or any other obligations to take care of. You're in great financial shape. This is just fun money. Close your eyes and imagine spending it on only spur-of-the-moment items. You could go to the fanciest restaurant in town. You can buy clothes that you'll wear only once and then donate them to charity. How about getting outrageously priced toys for the kids? You can buy whatever fun thing you want—as long as it's $500 or less. Use your imagination. Did you spend it? I'm sure you did. Do it again. Picture doing this every single day for thirty days. Remember that the money is for fun—not anything practical. Honestly now, it's becoming quite a challenge to think of things every day to buy for fun, isn't it? You're probably thinking, "I'd rather have that challenge than the debt any day!"

Well, if you had a million dollars piled up in a room, not even earning interest or dividends, it would take you *five and a half years* to spend it at the rate of $500 a day. At $1,000 a day it would take two years and nine months of nothing but fun spending!

Take it a step further. What if you were a billionaire? How long would it take you to spend that much money at $1,000 a day? I'll spell it out. *Two thousand seven hundred and fifty years!*

HOW ELSE COULD WEALTH AFFECT YOUR LIFE?

Let's take a different look at wealth. Being wealthy could be described as having peace of mind about your finances, right? How about having the financial freedom to live the life you want, knowing your future is secure? You no longer need to be concerned about spending too much money because your debt is gone. You can now easily afford to pay your expenses, do what you want to do, and you're no longer sacrificing your future due to the old debt. Isn't wealth simply not having to deal with what might be the number one concern among people today—money!

If you owned your home free and clear, had no debt, had money in the bank and a source of continuing income (job, business, or investments), would you be getting upset over money matters? Would you worry about how you'd pay for an unexpected repair on the family car? Of course not. You'd just write a check and pay for it. And *that* is what wealth and, more important, *financial freedom* is all about.

Wealth is having considerably more than what you need to survive. Our first example showed us that because of debt, $50,000 was needed to survive. Without debt, only $31,700 was needed. Which means the other $18,300 that comes in creates wealth. Solid wealth. Not paper equity that is only for people with a mortgage to help them feel better about owing money. This is liquid cash. As long as you've set aside what you need for a secure future (especially if you still have a job), you can spend it, invest it, or give it away with no negative consequences.

Do you now see wealth a bit differently? Does it seem more reachable? Once you're debt-free, it's likely that considerably less will be needed to maintain your lifestyle, which simply means you have more options. You can more easily see early retirement as a possibility for you. You can send the kids to college, if you want to, without putting yourself or them deeply in debt. I don't know about you, but to me, that's wealth and true financial freedom.

WEALTH MEANS CONTROL

Whoever controls the wealth, controls! Think about it. If you owe money, you're not in total control. In fact, if you're like many people, who are so deep in debt that they can't see their way out, you're out of control. Most everything you do (or don't do) is dictated by the ball and chain of debt. Where you *have to* work, how much you *have to* make, where you *have to* live, and so on, are determined by what you owe. The beauty of it, though, is that it's a do-it-yourself process. This means that it's also an undo-it-yourself process! You're in the driver's seat.

Before you're financially free, if you feel like rewarding yourself with a new car but you owe more on your old one than it is worth, it's possible you just can't afford to do it. The choice is basically made *for* you because of the financial choices you've made in the past. You would have to keep the car you're driving until it's paid for. What's amazing is that even while knowing this, 80 percent of the car buyers (in the States) still go out and *do it to themselves again!*

Say you owe nothing on your car, you've been making car-payment-sized deposits in your bank account each month for a while, and you later decide it's time to change. You could probably go into most car showrooms and choose what you *want* instead of *settling for* another monthly payment. Remember, *you can't drive a payment*. You can only drive the car—which again wouldn't really be yours. It would largely belong to the bank!

Are you ready to move on from that scenario? You're outgrowing it, aren't you?

IF THERE WERE ONLY ONE QUESTION TO ASK

As you create a wealth-inducing line of thinking, you'll need to change any debt-inducing habits you've acquired. It'll require effort—but you can do it. Having financial freedom as your goal is a great start. It'll give you hope as you encounter challenges. But what if you could ask yourself one important question that would help you stay on track before you transact any money? Would you do it? Here's the question: "Would you buy it that way if you were wealthy?"

Asking yourself that one question could help you make the right decision before deciding to commit any of your money to something. Creating the *thought process* that will occur when you ask yourself this question will help you *focus on where you're going* and avoid what could possibly keep you from getting there.

If the answer to the question is no, then you're better off not doing it. The reason is that chances are, if you've done it or something like it in the past, that action may well be one of the things that has held you back from the freedom you're now seeking to achieve.

For example, think back to the beginning of the book and the example of what charging some furniture really cost you. Would you have proceeded in the transaction if you had asked this question: "Would I pay for it this way if I were wealthy"? Probably not. The decision to charge the furniture could end up costing thousands of dollars more than the furniture was worth.

Would a wealthy person spend more on something than it was worth? Not if they plan to stay wealthy! Being and staying wealthy requires a certain attitude and a habit. Wealthy people don't simply throw money away. They're very conscious of it and its value in time.

The other thing asking questions like that will do is *open your mind to possibilities*. Perhaps there's a way for you to raise the cash for the purchase that you hadn't thought of before. If you had never asked yourself the question, you would've been closing your mind to other options. But if you asked the question and remained open-minded, you may figure out a way to do it that'll keep you on track. Wow! You then open yourself to a world of possibilities. Now, instead of charging something and going more deeply in debt, you're beginning to *think wealthy*. You begin to seek creative ways to come up with the money to get the things you had been charging in the past.

Another benefit to asking questions like this is that you can eliminate impulse buying. Have you ever bought something on impulse which you found you didn't really use once you got it home? Unfortunately, you were still paying on it for months (even years) to come. When you *pause for a moment* and ask yourself if you would do this if you were wealthy, sometimes you realize you wouldn't do it at all! In that instance, no purchase is made, and you didn't waste any money either.

Next you'll learn how to set yourself up to continue *thinking wealth* and actually put it into practice. You'll discover that not only is it simple, but when you stick to it for just 30 days, you'll see how much fun it is. You'll be encouraged to keep going until you're free. Remember, as George Matheson once said, "We conquer by continuing."

For most folks, the journey to being debt-free is like walking a thousand miles. But, as a Chinese philosopher pointed out, every journey begins with the first step. Turn the page and begin taking your first steps. Each one you take will bring you closer to the fulfillment of your dream of financial freedom, which you deserve.

PART TWO

THE MULTIPLE ACCOUNT PRINCIPLES

Today 20% of college students carry credit card balances of over $10,000.

Parade Magazine

CHAPTER SIX

Why Multiple Accounts?

Every man is the architect of his own fortune.

Sallust

WE GET WHAT WE THINK ABOUT!

If you were a bank teller, and I walked in with several account books with deposits for each, what would your reaction be? If I were well dressed, what would you think? That I might be worth some money—right? After all, if someone needs several accounts, it's logical to conclude that they must have at least *some* wealth.

Now, some banks charge fees until your balance reaches a certain level. Don't let this discourage you from setting up multiple accounts. Find a bank or credit union that has either low fees for their accounts or none at all. This is a big step in taking control of your finances. You need to find an institution that will help your money work for you. Paying fees isn't part of the program. Shop around. To do this, we first need to train our mind to think in terms of finance—in other words, smart money management. One of the early rules is to *never pay for something that you can get for free if you wait.*

By opening a savings account along with your checking account, you'll have the tools you need in place. Simply ask the bank for a few extra checking account registers (the books used to keep track of your balance). Label these with the names of the accounts that follow and deposit your money accordingly. (There are tables in the back of the book that you can use for each of your accounts.) Once you reach certain levels in each account (when it would pay you more to move the money elsewhere) then you can decide where to deposit it.

From this point forward, I'll be discussing the accounts that I have opened with my wife. It's best that you follow these steps on paper at first, and then ultimately, as we discussed earlier, in actual accounts when you meet or exceed the minimum amount required to incur no fees. It's simple to make the entries as we did, and to discipline yourself to use the on-paper accounts and the balances in them as I suggest. If you make mistakes in the process, learn from them, regain your focus, and get back on track. It gets easier as you develop new wealth-inducing thinking and habits. Have fun with it!

HOW WE STARTED

When my wife and I first began our journey towards financial freedom, we went to our bank to open the accounts you will learn about in the coming chapters. When we announced that we wanted to open six new accounts, they took us to a private office, gave us coffee, and treated us like preferred customers. Even when we were finished with our business, and they realized we hadn't deposited much money, the manager saw we were on to something. We've been preferred customers ever since.

When you put these ideas into action and experience this process, you'll understand how this simple but powerful multiple account system works. You will begin feeling wealthy as you make your trip to the bank for the first time to open your savings account (unless you already have one). You're preparing for the day when the banker *comes to you!* Once you get to a certain financial position, the bank will want to borrow money from you to loan out to others. It's likely they'll pay you more interest, depending on the sum you have invested with them in a money management type of account. It gets *very* interesting as you go along.

If the bank doesn't treat you like the customer you're becoming, *fire the bank!* That's right, let the bank know that you're searching for a place to put your money so that when you are financially free, you can just enjoy life and the money will keep rolling in—whether you work or not. If you sense that the institution isn't service-oriented and isn't interested in what you're doing, how do you know the bank will handle you properly when you are more successful?

Demonstrate that you are in control of your financial destiny. Take charge—question any policies that you don't like. Be a leader who's confident in your ability to make things happen for yourself and your family. When you find the place where you feel comfortable leaving your money, that confidence will radiate to the person serving you. You're laying the foundation for when you open actual multiple accounts. The branch manager may greet you, too. Be sure to enjoy the coffee or tea!

These practices are important for two reasons. First, it will be easier to manage your money when you have only a small amount. You won't feel the pressure of risking a bad decision with only a few dollars at stake. Get used to having things the way you'd like them to be and you'll find it easier to deal with opportunities or emergencies that come up.

Second, regardless of how much or little you have, the bank is obligated to serve you. You are the client. If the bank isn't taking great care of you now, why would you reward it later on when your money means a significant amount of profit potential for the bank? Don't reward poor service. Take total control of your future from the very beginning. After all, that's where you'll be spending the rest of your life.

WHY NOT JUST ONE ACCOUNT ON PAPER?

How has your having one account worked so far? Chances are you haven't achieved financially what you want from it. Whenever something isn't working, and you're not getting the results you want, change is in order. When I explain why each of the recommended accounts is necessary, you'll understand that you will achieve your goals in some of them much faster than in others. When your savings are broken out on paper, however, it's easier for you to feel a sense of accomplishment, which helps you to persistently continue on your journey.

The other reason for more than one account is faster growth. You need to see progress, which will motivate you to keep going. When you eliminate a bill, the monthly payments you were making will go into these other accounts. You'll be paying *yourself* instead of the bank! As this happens you will notice that your accounts begin growing at a faster rate. You're then making yourself rich instead of just pouring your hard-earned money into interest, which slows down, or even totally inhibits, your ability to get free of the bondage of loans. That then gives you the incentive to pay off more bills to get these accounts growing at an even faster pace.

It's an upward financial growth-producing spiral, which is one of the reasons the rich often get richer. If you have only one account on paper and do mental arithmetic, without recording it, as you pay off your bills, nothing changes. (That's why you need the check registers to track your money until you can open the other fee-free accounts.) If you just do it in your head, the money goes into and out of the same account, and you don't see any progress—on paper or in actuality. Again, to get different results, you need to do something different! (This sounds simple—and it is—but all of us need to move from having a great idea into taking action, if we expect to make a significant positive change in our financial picture, or in anything else, for that matter.)

Having multiple accounts can spur you on to accomplish your goals. You'll feel like you're doing something positive about your financial predicament—and you *are*! You'll feel encouraged to keep going and continue your savings program. I have done this countless times in my head and found it ineffective—until I began the multiple account practice.

When I used to keep track of the savings in my head, using only one account, I thought I was disciplined enough to succeed. In one sense I was. I had disciplined myself to believe that every time an emergency occurred (which seemed like whenever I wanted something), I could take the money out and spend it. I would console myself by saying that I had already proven I could save once, therefore I could do it again. Sound familiar? I used to fool myself time and time again.

Another reason for the multiple account method is favoritism. As your accounts grow, one of them might excite you more than the others. When this happens, you can shift the allocations (detailed later) and put more money into that particular account. You couldn't get that same feeling of accomplishment if you hadn't designated your money, on paper at least, into several accounts.

WHERE DOES THIS MONEY COME FROM?

Up to this point, things may *sound* great. Having several accounts with money getting deposited and growing is great in theory, but you're probably asking yourself, where does all this money come from? I did. When I first learned this method of successful financial freedom, I wondered, "Since I don't have the money to save in *just one* account, where will the money come from to fill multiple accounts?"

The answer almost caused me to walk away from this idea immediately. "It's been there all along." Imagine how I felt hearing that! I'm going nowhere financially, looking for a solution and a future, and now I'm told it's been there all along. Please. But you know what? As you continue to have the patience to complete this book you will see that that's *exactly* where it is—right under your nose.

Picture this. Say you've been a loyal, hardworking employee for 15 years. Suppose tomorrow you go to work and the boss calls you into his or her office. He or she announces that even though you are a valuable part of the company, the firm is cutting your pay by 10 percent, along with everyone else's, so that the company can survive. Could you still pay all your bills and maintain your current standard of living? If you're honest with yourself, in all likelihood, the answer is yes.

Here's another scenario: What if you lose your job unexpectedly and the best you can do is replace 90 percent of your income? Does that sound more possible? It's basically the same thing—just a different way of looking at it!

Right now either of those situations could cause a temporary hardship on you and your family. That's mainly because either would be a surprise. You probably aren't prepared for such a turn of events, are you? Suppose you were ready for it—how would you feel then? By following what comes next, not only will you be prepared for just such an occurrence—you'll actually prosper in the process!

WHERE *NOT* TO PUT ALL YOUR EGGS

Having a few accounts with specific intentions for each will help you solve short-term financial problems a lot more quickly. When you have a special account set up *just* for debt elimination (you'll see how to use it in later chapters), the tendency is to use the money only for that purpose. Similarly, having an account dedicated to saving money for investments reduces the likelihood of your spending it on other things.

When you're at the stage where you only have one account and you're investing the little bit of time it takes to separate the money on paper into individual accounts, it's much easier than trying to keep all the separate amounts in your head. Plus, when you have an undesignated lump sum, it's easier for you to justify spending because there's plenty left. In other words, you could be more tempted to spend money on a big-ticket fun item when your money's in one account with no set purposes than when the same money is split among several actual or on-paper accounts.

For many people, the incentive of watching several accounts grow at the same time is enough to keep them on the program. The safety net here is, if an emergency should occur so that you can't put as much into all the accounts, you can make different decisions. You can decide that each gets a smaller amount or that some accounts get nothing this time while your favorites get their usual contribution. You're in charge! And controlling your destiny is almost as important as eliminating debt from your life.

MONEY VERSUS FINANCE

Having multiple accounts also helps you to shift your mind to a wealth-inducing attitude. It's a thinking-bigger level that many people have never reached, simply because they have thought primarily of getting by week to week so they can pay their bills. They're in a survival mode—living from paycheck to paycheck, with no reserves. Most people don't think in terms of finance. Finance (not to be confused with financing, i.e., borrowing to purchase) is defined by *Webster's New Universal Unabridged Dictionary* as "the management of revenues; the conduct or transaction of money matters generally, especially those affecting the public; as in the fields of banking and investment. . . ." It's a bigger arena than money, and therein lies the difference.

We think of money often in terms of what we can buy, what we earn, or how much is in our pockets or checking account at any given time. Finance, on the other hand, has to do with banks, institutions and *the wealthy*. Finance is big numbers, money changing hands at the speed of light, investments growing right before our eyes. It's the rich getting richer. But most of us never seem to see finance as something *we're* involved in.

The exciting news is, that's all about to change. *Having multiple accounts gets you involved with finance*. Regardless of how much is in those accounts, they can grow and help to set you free once you accept the power of finance over money.

People in debt need money. People who are free deal in finance and gain wealth. Where do you want to be?

Do you realize that the Federal Deposit Insurance Corporation (FDIC) in the United States insures accounts only up to $100,000? When you actually approach this amount in a couple or more of your actual accounts, you're all set. They're all insured. When you're financially secure, you'll establish multiple accounts to deal with the excess. (By then you may have a financial advisor who suggests you invest some of your funds elsewhere. It's likely you'll be in a position to risk some of it for higher returns.) Act as if you're wealthy and do as the wealthy do. Begin with this multiple savings account approach—it is real and it works!

Having multiple accounts helps you to gain more control of your finances. You have several sums of money to use for a variety of purposes. As you learn the ways to use each account, you'll understand that some have specific objectives, while others allow you the freedom that you may have thought came only from using credit cards.

You will begin making *financial decisions* rather than just everyday money decisions. What that means is you'll be thinking beyond your immediate short-term needs. You'll be thinking long-term as well—for your future—as you make each spending or investing decision. *No more basing purchasing decisions on whether you can afford the monthly payments*. That's short-term thinking that leads to long-term regret. From now on you look at the total cost or savings that results from a thoughtful *financial* decision.

When you see everything from not only the immediate gratification side but also from the consequence or future side, money becomes a tool to serve *you* rather than you forever being in bondage and serving it. Finance takes money out of your focus and puts it under your control—where it belongs. You will see that with the accounts I recommend, should you decide to use them, you will *always* have money. It's up to you whether you're serious enough to turn the corner toward financial freedom.

The reason always having money is important is *control*. If you are without money, the need for it controls you and rules your life. Much of your thinking will focus around money—either having it, getting it, earning it, or figuring out how to keep your creditors happy month to month. But when you are in a situation where you always have money, *you* are in control—you're in the driver's seat. You will never again worry about being broke, who to pay this month and how much, or where the next dollar will come from. You won't be bouncing checks and cringing because you can't afford to pay the bank's insufficient funds charges, which may be even higher than the bill you aren't able to pay—or so you think. Since you will be creating a situation where you'll always have money, you can focus on what you need to concentrate on. Instead of worrying about money, you can devote time to creating financial freedom. That, to me, is worth whatever effort it takes. How about you?

Are you sick and tired of being sick and tired of the strain of living from paycheck to paycheck? Do you realize how much energy you're using just to cope with your money situation? The great news is you can break free, and I'm here to guide you through it.

Conquering any difficulty always gives one a secret joy, for it means pushing back a boundary line and adding to one's liberty.

Henri Frederic Amiel

If you're looking for a big opportunity, seek out a big problem.

Unknown

CHAPTER SEVEN

The Cash Flow Account

Any dream can be achieved with the right attitude, focus, consistent action, and persistence.

John Fuhrman

DOES IT SEEM TO BE SPENT BEFORE YOU GET IT?

Have you ever felt the dissatisfaction that occurs after working all week and getting a check, only to know it's already been spent?

Many people believe that never having enough money is normal because most of their friends are in the same boat. So they commiserate together about being broke and they fail to take action. They keep on doing what they've been doing—maintaining the same pattern of behavior that led to their money challenges in the first place. They keep repeating the same mistakes, getting themselves deeper and deeper in debt.

One technique that many speakers and trainers use to break habits is called "pattern interrupt." It does what it sounds like. When you're in a pattern of habitual behavior, you act almost unconsciously—that is, without thinking. You go through the motions, practically unaware that you're doing it. It can be almost robotic. In fact, in the case of your paycheck, you may be habitually dreading payday and facing the fact that even though you're working hard, you're not able to make ends meet. You may have accepted this as your plight, believing there's nothing you can do about it.

For the purposes of creating wealth, your pattern interrupt is the *Cash Flow* account. This account breaks the cycle and slows down the old spending process. You're beginning a new habit that begins to put you back in control of your money. You'll start to see yourself change from being almost unconscious about your expenditures—from almost passively wondering where your money goes each month—to taking charge and dealing with *finance*.

In all likelihood, you are already noticing that your attitude is shifting from accepting the state of being broke, or close to it, as a way of life, to that of renewed hope. You're realizing that you can, for once and for all, throw off the shackles of financial bondage. You can achieve whatever you decide to go for, including financial freedom, as long as you keep persisting—doing whatever it takes. Other people have done it, and you can too!

CHANGE YOUR MIND ABOUT MONEY

Another aspect of managing and acquiring wealth is that you need to change how you feel about money. Thinking you don't have enough, thinking you're not being paid what you're worth, thinking other people have all the money—these are all just thoughts. Your thoughts control how you act around money. It's an inside (your mind) job.

I could spend chapters quoting mind experts like Napoleon Hill in his book *Think and Grow Rich*, Dr. Shad Helmstetter's *What to Say When You Talk to Yourself*, and Maxwell Maltz's *Psycho-Cybernetics*, but you can explore those resources on your own. Right now it's important for you to consider where you are financially. Then let's take a look at your thoughts regarding money.

Some people grew up being told that rich people were really miserable and that money couldn't buy happiness. You may have been told that money is the root of all evil. The first thing you need to understand is that money is an inanimate object. It is simply a medium of exchange. We exchange it for food, clothing, shelter, and other items. While I agree it can't buy happiness, I would have to add that money, in and of itself, couldn't cause misery either! Money is not the root of all evil. In the Bible it says, "The *love* of money is the root of all evil."

I believe there may be a different meaning of love in the previous quote. I believe that love is meant as an overriding power, a control you don't have. In other words, you are controlled by money. *That is what debt does to you!* It puts you in a position where every move you make revolves around money—where you live, what you must do for work, when you can retire.

You need to *stop making money the excuse for the way you feel about where you are in your life*. You need the freedom to do what you love rather than what you have to do because money (debt) *controls* you. *That, in my opinion, is the root of all evil!*

One way to do that is to recognize money for what it is. It's a tool—a tool that *you can use and control.* You need to control it, not the other way around. Think of a hammer. When you use it correctly, you can build things. You control where and what it strikes. That control in your hands can create or destroy something. Can a hammer ever control you? Can it dictate to you where to hit or make you build an inferior project? Of course not. It's the same way with money. It can't make you do anything. It's up to you what you do or don't do with it.

There's no question that it takes effort to change your thoughts (beliefs) and the habits that you've developed based on these thoughts. Anything worthwhile, though, takes effort. Your mind is a very powerful part of you. It may resist letting go of the habits that it is used to. In fact, when you begin to make an effort to change your thinking directly, introducing ideas that are different than you're accustomed to entertaining, your mind may resist these ideas. This happens because your subconscious has held a different belief system.

In this case, your beliefs, some of which may be false, have led you to create your current money situation. Your thinking controls your life. Once you're an adult, anything or anybody else who you believe controls you can only do so because, at some level, you've allowed them to. When we really get it that we're in charge of our own well-being, miracles can happen as we learn to make better choices each day and take the action required to carry out our new decisions.

The direct approach of attempting to change your subconscious mind is only temporarily effective, at best. You need to change your thinking at the subconscious level. So what do you need to do to make this process as simple and effective as possible?

TEACH YOUR SUBCONSCIOUS AFFIRMATIONS

Perhaps you've heard of affirmations. You may even have an opinion of them. Some of you may believe they don't work. That's okay. Hang on for a bit. Maybe this will change your perspective.

First, affirmations are not just mindless repetitions of words where, as in the Disney movie *Peter Pan*, we think happy thoughts and can then fly. Affirmations are positive statements designed to help us change our thinking to what we'd like it to be in order to get the results we want. They not only work but, whether we realize it or not, most of us have used them all our lives! For me, it was back in Little League. "See the ball hit the bat," my coach said over and over. I began saying it to myself, and, eventually, I began hitting.

Affirmations demonstrate the tremendous power of the mind. Here's an example you may relate to. If you're still not convinced, try this. What if for the next 30 days, just before you go to bed, you'd spend five minutes thinking about getting a serious illness? You are undoubtedly taken aback by the mere thought of doing this to yourself—and rightly so.

Most of you wouldn't do that, and I certainly don't recommend it. It's likely that you realize that it is possible to think yourself sick.

Why is it most of us believe the negative things our mind can do, but many of us don't realize the positive things it can do? It works the same way; affirmations are equally powerful when used for beneficial purposes. Any thought, true or false, positive or negative, repeated over and over, becomes a belief, then a reality. Your subconscious is not able to tell if what it's being told is accurate or inaccurate. In the final analysis, the bottom line is that your life reflects your thinking. This is a key point to remember.

Once your mind takes possession of something, it doesn't let go. Every thought you've ever had, true or false, beneficial or detrimental, is somewhere inside your subconscious mind. What affirmations do is dilute and overpower the detrimental beliefs and habits. The letting go of old ideas and constant repetition of the new ideas will weaken the hold of the thoughts that cause a habit until it is a distant and unconscious memory. It's just like if I told you to drink a pint of vinegar and you'll get rich. Just the thought would turn most people away. To the majority, vinegar has a strong, unpleasant taste. But what if you were to pour it into a 55-gallon barrel of crystal clear, pure spring water. Wouldn't it be easier to drink?

Throughout this book I will be adding affirmations to help you begin thinking in ways that will be financially beneficial to you now and in the future. When you participate in this process for 30 days, you can create new habits that will support you in becoming debt-free and, as you persist, even financially free, depending on how serious you are about making it happen.

Write your affirmations down and say them out loud before you go to bed every night. This way, as you sleep, they can become engrained in your mind without having to compete with all the other thoughts you have during the day. I recommend that you allow yourself 10 minutes or so before you go to bed, and write the affirmations on a piece of paper 20 times every night. You can also write the affirmations in large print on a sheet of paper and hang it where you'll see it often—perhaps in your bathroom, on your refrigerator, or by your bed. Some people also record their affirmations on an audiocassette tape and listen to them daily. The first one is, "I always have more money than I need."

The reason the affirmation is stated in the present tense is that it is the truth in advance. If you always affirm that something will happen in the future, it always remains a future event!

If you find that as you're writing the affirmations, contradictory thoughts are in your mind, write down those thoughts on another sheet of paper. When you cease to have contradictory thoughts, that means your subconscious mind has accepted the new idea as true for you. This happens as you persistently affirm what you want.

Another point regarding affirmations: They are only effective when you are the person who is to take action. For example, if you say, "(Your spouse's name) always has more money than he (she) needs," it won't work! You could, however, use "We" as long as you and your spouse are both affirming it!

TAKING ONLY WHAT YOU NEED

Do you cash your paycheck, go grocery shopping, figure out the bills, and put what you need in the checking account, only to be broke again within 48 hours or less? If that's your routine each time you're paid, you're not alone. Many people are in the same boat. They pay the rent or mortgage with the last paycheck of the month. They string out paying the car insurance over however many months their insurance company lets them. They have one or more car payments, on loans that are stretched out over several years, like small mortgage payments—or maybe not so small. They always seem to get a bill and *then* chase the money.

If you have no financial direction, your money ends up

everywhere but with you. You end up making the financial institutions rich—rather than yourself. I hope that you follow the suggestions offered here, take control of your money, and create financial freedom. You'll be glad you did.

The first thing to do is put all the money you receive into the Cash Flow account. This can be a checking or savings account. The first benefit to you is that you are making the transition to finance, because when you have a savings or checking account that pays interest and you use it properly, the bank is *working for you*. But understand that this account is not for your savings. It is simply the beginning of your financial structure. You may want to use a savings account because it generally pays more interest than a checking account and typically has a lower fee. However, since the money in this account generally doesn't stay there long enough to generate significant earnings, the convenience of a checking account that pays interest may be better suited to your needs.

There are other benefits to this account. You will be able to keep track of all the personal income you receive during the course of the year because all your earnings are deposited into this account. This will provide you with a clear record for tax purposes and for comparisons as to how you're doing from month to month. It will create some extra work and show you that finance takes effort, but the rewards are great. This process will eliminate the "something-for-nothing" mindset, which will help keep you going even when it seems challenging. Anything worthwhile takes effort.

The final benefit is control. What makes this process work is that *you* consciously dictate the flow of *your* money. When you deposit money into this account, let it sit there for at least 24 hours. Enjoy the fact that your paycheck (and your spouse's too, if you're married and your spouse has a job) is sitting in the bank. Your money can't go anywhere unless you release it! Isn't that great? This will help you be more aware of your money outgo and reduce any feelings that your money is just slipping through your fingers without your permission.

PAY THE MOST IMPORTANT PERSON IN YOUR LIFE

I understand that depressing feeling after payday—all that work, and the money is already gone. You feel like you're just grinding it out without any true sense of satisfaction. I know—I've been there. While I believe that any obligation you incur is your responsibility, I maintain that you are also entitled to be rewarded for your labor. In fact, you should be rewarded first!

Remember when we discussed the possibility of making 10 percent less during a cutback at work or from losing your job and getting another job? That's what we're going to do now. Only the 10 percent you "lose" from the Cash Flow account will be going right to your future. You will be putting it into the accounts that will be explained in coming chapters.

For some of you, losing that 10 percent may seem difficult at first, and it may take time to get used to it. That's okay. Any discomfort is likely to be temporary. What will happen is that as you see the other accounts growing, you will find it not only easier but even exciting! You will look forward to each payday just to continue building your *finances* while *not* worrying about money.

Perhaps, after a short time, you will find that your new habit of setting aside 10 percent for yourself is no problem, especially as you begin reducing your debt. That's fine. I recommend 10 percent as a minimum. As you read and understand the purposes of each account, you may decide to put more aside in order to achieve your individual goals more quickly.

Some of you receive windfalls every now and then. They may be inheritances, bonuses, gifts, commissions, or other forms of non-wage income. You can split this money any way you like. It can certainly be done by the formula, but as my accounts started to grow and I became excited, I would often put all of it into the accounts you are going to read about. That gave all of them a tremendous boost—and gave me a great incentive to keep going.

These accounts are not the only ones that you can use. We will mention others later on. These are simply recommendations that worked for me and for others I have shared this program with as well. You may have different needs and goals. This approach will give you ideas to consider so you can create your own special accounts.

To have money is a good thing; to have say over money is even better.

Yiddish Proverb

Who has lost his freedom has nothing left to lose.

German Proverb

CHAPTER EIGHT

The Permanent Wealth Account

People who build wealth think differently than those who don't. . . . The millionaire mindset is simple: It's not what you make that counts. It's what you keep.

Michael LeBoeuf

A NEW FEELING OF SECURITY

How would you feel if you saw an ad in the paper that guaranteed you'd never be broke again? Would you believe it? Many people would begin looking for the catch, thinking that there must be something wrong, costly, or even illegal. Why? Why is it that we may not believe something that could bring us happiness, yet we swallow all the negative information the media dishes out?

As long as you have that sense of doubt in the back of your mind about any opportunity to make some positive changes, you will limit your growth. I'm not asking you to accept everything as total truth as advertised. Healthy skepticism is one thing, and certainly you need to use discretion, but disbelieving anything good is another. If you find yourself regularly resisting any possibility you're offered to make some necessary changes, stop and examine why. You need to dilute that negative thought process. In this case, ask yourself if you're serious about creating financial freedom and security. Are you open-minded and teachable? Here's another affirmation to help you move in the right direction: *I always look for ways to have money work for me.*

How much is more than enough? For your thought process, the amount doesn't matter. Still, as long as you have money that you'll never touch, you'll *always have more than enough*. But, you may ask, isn't that like giving it away? If you can never use it, what good is it? Be patient. This account could become your favorite one!

Have you ever seen a wealthy person on the news or in the paper? Have you ever said that you'd be happy just to live off the interest they're earning? Well, that's exactly what the *Permanent Wealth* account will become. And you'll find that you can have a lot of fun along the way.

For now, though, you need to begin by adding your new affirmation to your daily routine: *I always look for ways to have money work for me*. You need to build a strong wealth-inducing belief system before the money comes. Proceed with the confidence that you can do it. Trust the process and, again, be patient.

You need to have a big *dream* or a goal (a dream with a deadline) before you can accomplish it. It will help you intensify your desire. Also, without a big dream or goal, what would you need more money for? Simply to pay off bills? That isn't a tangible, exciting goal to shoot for. Strive to achieve your big dream—whether it's a new house, a vacation, college of the kid's choice, or something else—and pay your bills off as you go towards it. It's important to be going towards something that you really, really want. This, of course, applies to anything worthwhile, not just money.

WHY IS THE PERMANENT WEALTH ACCOUNT SO POWERFUL?

Since you're reading this book, your first deposit into this account probably won't be a million dollars. So what makes this account so important to your future? While the other accounts you'll learn about are also important, this account is not only a tool you can use to create your financial future but, of all the accounts, it is also the best teacher of finance.

Another affirmation you need to begin saying each night is, *I'm creating wealth 24 hours a day, 365 days a year*. While the other affirmations take time, this one begins working instantly. As soon as you put money in this or any of the other accounts, it begins earning interest. That means you are earning money every minute of every day, whether you're working, playing, or even sleeping. You're shifting from a spending mentality to a wealth-building mentality. *That's finance!*

As this account grows in size, you will be looking for better ways to invest it. You will want and be qualified for a greater return on your money. When this happens, you'll be well on your way to independence. As the rate of interest you can earn increases, you'll receive more earnings for the same amount of money. By moving it to where it can earn more, you have taken control of your money. It's a great feeling!

People who have money working for them are in control. Those who are deep in debt, with no savings, are almost totally controlled by money—or rather, the lack of it. Part of financial freedom is not how much you have but rather, who's in control. This account teaches control.

When you are in control of your finances, freedom could very well be close at hand. Remember, first it has to happen mentally, then it can happen physically. Napoleon Hill, in his classic book *Think and Grow Rich*, shares, "Truly, thoughts are things, and powerful things at that, when they are mixed with definiteness of purpose, persistence, and a burning desire for their translation into riches or other material objects."

THE FUN OF FINANCE

The first lesson I learned was what I call *never less than*. Whatever you put into your Permanent Wealth account will always be there. It will never be spent for anything. Here's what I mean. Let's say you are able to contribute $5 a week into this account. By the end of three months you'd have approximately $70 in the account. You could then tell yourself that no matter what happens, you'd never have less than $70. At the end of a year of contributing $5 each week, as before, you'd then be able to say that no matter what happens, you'll never have less than $260. After two years, $520. And so on. You will discover that your ability to generate money will also increase in those increments.

Can you imagine yourself beginning to feel more secure about your money? With each passing contribution, you're setting new limits for yourself. As the accounts grow, they become your new minimum standard. They are like a protective wall you build, brick by brick. In the beginning you won't be shielded by much but, with each contribution, you'll be getting closer to your goal of financial freedom.

While this may be a valuable lesson, I believe that for something to be learned well, it also needs to be fun. One of the fun things you can do with this account will also teach you a great deal about finance. When you set up this account, request that the bank mail you the earned interest every quarter. In the beginning the checks will probably be small, but the lesson they teach will be huge.

My first check was for an amount so small that the stamp to mail it to me almost cost as much. I had forgotten it was coming, and when it showed up in the mail, it took a moment for me to figure out what it was for. But that check was worth an enormous amount—enormous because I *did absolutely nothing* to earn it! Isn't that great? Many people have a "paycheck mentality." This is the attitude that money only comes from working hard at a job and trading your time for dollars. This thinking prevents people from accepting the fact that there are many legal ways to come into money other than by the sweat of their brow. Some of those ways even pay better! So let go of any paycheck mentality you may have and be open-minded to the many money-generating possibilities.

That check proved to me that I could receive money without having to work for it. When I controlled the money, rather than the other way around, I was dealing in finance. When you deal in finance, the money is working for you instead of you working for the money! I began to look for ways to increase the amount I was putting into this account (more about that later).

By the end of the year, the quarterly interest check that came in the mail was over $60! Not enough to retire on, but I still hadn't done anything to earn it! My money did all the work! If you were working at a part-time job making $5 an hour, you would have to work for 12 hours to earn as much as I received free in the mail—without working for it! Or, on the more positive side, you could work fewer hours, knowing that you already have the money coming in. If you earned $10 an hour, you could work six fewer hours and spend time with those you care about and still have that amount coming in.

Even at a rate of $20 an hour, you could still work three hours less. While that may not sound like much, imagine being able to take your daughter to a movie in the middle of the afternoon and really enjoy it rather than worrying about how to make up for the lost income.

The reason I'm sharing this experience with you is because small numbers are more believable. I believe you can see these results as possible for you. Once your money is working for you, almost by itself, you will start to get the incentive to help it along. Your creativity will begin to come up with ways to either earn more or spend less to help this account (and the others) grow. Once you can understand the concept using small numbers, it then becomes only a matter of repeating the process until you reach whatever level of financial security is right for you.

WHAT IS PERMANENT WEALTH?

What would you do if you received a check for $60 in the mail each quarter with absolutely no strings attached? It almost doesn't matter what the answer is. But what if you knew that you would continue getting a check for $60 without any effort on your part? How would you feel then?

You see, even if you stopped putting money into your Permanent Wealth account, the money would continue showing up in your mailbox. No matter what you did the rest of your life, that money would keep on coming. Wow! That's what financial freedom is all about.

In this example, I showed you that I achieved a level of $60 interest per quarter, after one year. How much you earn will depend on many factors—debt, current income, your level of contribution, and what interest rates you can earn. But for the sake of example, let's assume you are earning $60 each quarter, after one year. Let's also say you're 30 years old and you want to retire at age 50.

If you stopped the account at the end of the year and started over every January first with a new account until the age of 50, what would happen? Starting these accounts under the same conditions and interest rates would earn $60 per quarter for each account. At the age of 50 you would have 20 individual accounts, each paying $60 per quarter. (I would not recommend this many accounts; I use this number simply to demonstrate how finance can work for you. It would be better to keep this as one account, and when it reaches a large number you can seek the advice of a financial planner to get the best return.)

Every quarter you would receive a check for $1,200 based on $60 from each account (i.e., $4,800 a year)—whether you work or not! If you spent every dime of the checks that came in over the following years and had nothing to show for it, so what? At the end of the next quarter, here comes another check. This is just an illustration. What you'd probably do is build up the same account year after year until it reaches a point where it can work better for you in another vehicle.

Also, in order to keep things simple, I didn't use what many call the eighth wonder of the world—compound interest. That is where your money *really* works. You earn interest on the interest. That's like having your money work overtime for you!

What's even more amazing is, unlike your pension (if you're fortunate enough to have one), this money will never run out. You are only receiving the interest. The principal keeps on working for you. And the nice thing about money is, once you understand finance and learn to control it, it (your principal) *never* needs to retire! It'll keep on working for you as long as you continue to control it!

Let's look at another real possibility. Say that your earnings increase over the years. And as you follow the rest of this program and eliminate your debts, it makes sense that you'll be able to contribute more than the $5 a week minimum we gave you as an example. What if, over the years, you increase your contributions to your Permanent Wealth account, put some of the interest back into the account (or you don't withdraw all of it in the first place), and find places where the money would earn you more? It's possible you could receive quarterly checks that could equal or exceed your current income.

Imagine earning your income by having money work for you, rather than you working for it at a job. Think it's out of reach? Think again. This is only the first account you have set up for your journey toward true financial independence.

The examples that follow will be in small amounts. They are taken from the journals I kept when I started the process. Remember, I was deep in debt, had no savings program to speak of, and was looking for a way to provide for my family that would allow me to spend more time with them.

People are always blaming their circumstances for what they are. The people who get on in this world are they who get up and look for the circumstances they want, and, if they can't find them, make them.

George Bernard Shaw

Decisions determine destiny.

Frederick Speakman

Tomorrow is the most important thing in life.
Comes to us at midnight very clean. It's perfect
when it arrives and it puts itself in our hands.
It hopes we've learned something from
yesterday.

John Wayne

CHAPTER NINE

The Totally Fun Account

When the task is enjoyed the results are better and happen sooner.

John Fuhrman

THE REWARD SHOULD
EQUAL THE CONTRIBUTION

One of the ways many people, including myself, have tried to eliminate debt is by putting every penny into paying off all the bills. When people makes a decision like that, it's usually because they owe quite a bit more than they are comfortable with. They feel trapped and desperate. Often that causes them to go to extremes. They learn the truth of what someone once said: "He who borrows sells his freedom."

After charging and borrowing their way to instantly gratify their desire for good times, they begin to feel guilty. In a knee-jerk reaction, they inflict a financial punishment on themselves. No more fun and nice things until all the bills are paid for. No good times until they've punished themselves for past mistakes.

Imagine, if you will, getting deeper into debt over a two-year period. You make a decision to pay it off at all cost. Beginning today, nothing that could bring fun, pleasure, or convenience into your life will be bought until everything is paid for. No more charges, no more restaurant meals, no more vacations until you owe no money.

While getting free from debt is what this is about, staying free once you're there is equally important. This book is not about learning to get free of debt over and over. It's about doing it once while creating permanent wealth and financial security for you and your family—for life!

Now if you had sacrificed everything for two years to pay off your bills, how do you think you'd feel when you were done? Would you feel pleased (deservedly so) with your accomplishment and get on with your life? Or would part of you feel deprived—that you just worked for two solid years, spending all this energy and money, doing without, just to get to zero? More than likely, it's a mixture of both.

Sacrificing over an extended period, without reward, can lead to disappointment—a sense of deprivation. When you work hard to accomplish something, you are entitled to some benefit. Part of your mind sees the benefit of owing nothing, but the other part focuses on the nothing. If you're like most people, you have been conditioned with a paycheck mentality. That means when you perform a task, you expect that there will be compensation of some kind.

Many times your mind creates a logic you like to hear, so you may not argue with it. In this case, it might tell you to go ahead and reward yourself with something nice. Even if you have to charge it, your mind may rationalize (tell itself rational lies) that you should get it anyway. After all, you've proven you can get out of debt before, right? Or your mind may tell you that you need to stay clear of debt. That's great, but what about financial security, wealth? Just staying out of debt is key, but you undoubtedly want more than that, or you wouldn't be reading this book.

How do you train your mind not to want to charge things, but still provide times and gifts of enjoyment to your family and yourself? How do you break away from making a living into having a life, without running the credit cards up to the maximum? Is it ever going to get any better? Are you destined to always receive credit card bills in the mail?

DID YOU EVER DIET?

Statistics claim that 92 percent of people who diet gain back all the weight they lost; many gain even more. Why is that? I'm no authority on weight loss and diets, but I believe it can be explained. As I stated earlier, many of us have been conditioned to believe that loss is unpleasant and gain is good. When we diet, we focus on *losing* weight by *depriving* ourselves of the physical and mental pleasure of certain foods.

What if we approached it a little differently? For those of you carrying some extra pounds, what are all the *benefits* of reducing your weight? Better health, more energy, and self-esteem, to name just a few. You may have other reasons, but the point is to look at what you *gain*. When you concentrate on the personal gains from proper dieting, you focus on the positive. Once your mind is working in that direction and you're committed to your goal, a little treat, as a reward, won't keep you from your final destination. In fact, it will go a long way toward reducing the cravings from being deprived of treats like dessert.

That is the first benefit of the *Totally Fun* account. When you are putting aside money to reduce your debt, you're in the money frame of mind. When you have money that is destined to be spent for whatever you feel like buying, with *no guilt attached*, you are telling your mind that wealth and financial security are coming to you. That's finance.

SETUP

This account can be set up in one of two ways—either by amount or by time. Some people prefer to use this account every time they have a certain dollar amount in it. Let's say $100. Every time the account reaches that level, they can go shopping and spend up to $100 guilt-free.

Others set a time limit. Every so often, in a time frame they designate, they go fun-shopping with the money from that account. I prefer this method and use a 30-day time period. Either approach works, but for me this way adds a little more surprise. The reason is that my income fluctuates from month to month, so we never know how much will be there. This method also lets me know that after I work hard for a few weeks, there will be a pleasurable reward.

HOW TO DOUBLE YOUR FUN

The reason this is called the Totally Fun account is because the money can be used for any spur-of-the-moment purchase you want to make. It teaches you that once you reach the level of financial thinking, it's okay to spend for the sheer joy of it without feeling guilty. The whole purpose of the account is to allow you to do this without taking away from your other obligations.

Understand, you are *not* to overextend this account! You are limited to what it actually contains at the moment of the purchase. Never get something based on what you think may be in the account next month. You also should never preplan your fun shopping. The more spur-of-the-moment these future purchases are, the more impact they will have on creating *finance thinking* as opposed to money worrying.

When the day arrives to shop, bring only your account book with you. I suggest you shop where you've never been before. The first time my wife and I did this, we went to a roadway that was lined with antique and specialty shops. We went into these stores with about $60 to spend and were looking for anything that caught our eye (in other words, not looking at price tags).

We spotted an incredibly ugly vase. It reminded me of the distant relative who sends a wedding gift and then shows up to see where you put it. It never seems to fit anywhere. We had never gotten any ugly gifts, and we thought this would be a great conversation piece, if nothing else! The price however, was $80. Now we could have taken the other $20 from one of the other accounts, but we were determined to follow the rules and make this fun account idea work. So we offered the dealer $50 for the vase.

After a few minutes of haggling we agreed on $60. Perfect. We were excited. We learned how to negotiate, got our price, and didn't overspend our Totally Fun account limit. Now let's double our fun, positive feelings, and financial mindset.

Once we had agreed on the price, I took out my account book. (I never withdraw the money first. I leave it in the bank, working for me until the last minute.) I showed it to the dealer and briefly explained what my wife and I were doing. When I finished, I asked him if he would be willing to hold it for three days and I'd pick it up then. He agreed. (Had he not agreed, we would have just continued shopping at other stores until we found something else.)

As we drove home that day we had the exhilarating feeling of having plenty of money. We had "spent" the money without having to worry about where it would come from or what we would have to sacrifice in the future because of what we had done. We had negotiated for what we wanted, "purchased" it, and had the satisfaction of knowing our financial house was in order.

But wait. We didn't have the vase yet. We still had to go back again and pay for it. It wasn't going home with us that day. It was still sitting in the shop. That's true, but *mentally* we owned it. In our minds we had gone through the process and purchased it. What do you suppose we went through when we returned to pick it up a few days later?

We went through the entire process again. We felt the

excitement and the security of dealing in finance all over again! It proved the system works. Twice! If the best way to learn is through repetition, you'll have the benefits of this account engrained in your mind in half the time, because every time you use this account, you'll be doing it twice.

WHAT YOU THINK ABOUT HAPPENS

Let's say that for several months you've been enjoying the benefits of having this account. Each time you clear it out, that purchase triggers a thought process. The price of the purchase stays with you during the two or three days before you pick it up. When that dollar amount is in your head for those days, your mind begins getting creative.

When you begin thinking of finances and money in a positive and creative sense, more of it will show up in your life. Now I'm not talking about money magically appearing, but you'll be amazed at how you'll begin attracting money after doing the Totally Fun account process for a while. It took me about seven months to notice the difference.

At that time I had worked my way up to having about $250 in the account. As was now the tradition, we went shopping on a Saturday and came across an item that ended up costing $225. We got the storeowner to agree to hold it for us until Wednesday. On my way to pick it up, I looked in the mailbox and found two checks totaling $225!

One of the checks was for money that someone had owed me for such a long time that I had written it off, and the other was for a refund that I wasn't expecting for weeks. Pretty lucky, huh? Well I believe that luck is a result of hard (and smart) work, which puts you in a position where opportunity and preparedness come together. Focus and concentrate on specifics, and you're more likely to achieve your goals.

The life each of us lives is the life within the limits of our own thinking. To have life more abundant, we must think in limitless terms of abundance.

Thomas Dreier

There is no growth except in the fulfillment of obligations.

Anonymous

CHAPTER TEN

The Future Growth Account

When you begin building your future today, you'll have a positive effect on how you'll be able to live five years from now.

Unknown

WILL YOU MAKE ENOUGH?

At some point in everyone's life, the question about the future arises. As you have things set up now, when you retire, will there be enough money for you to live on and do what you want to do? With people living longer on average, that question becomes very important. I believe if you rely on your earnings to get you through, you'll be in danger of having to live out the remainder of your life constantly cutting back.

To me that doesn't seem right. You put in your time at a career, working for the day when you can retire and enjoy life. Why should you have to sell your home and cut back on travel plans many times just to make ends meet? Probably because your time was spent thinking about money instead of using finance to build your future.

Usually it's dangerous to make assumptions, but I believe if you've read this far, it's likely you haven't put much away for the future. In fact you keep looking toward the future, rarely realizing that today is the future you were looking at a few months or years ago. Financially, if you look back five years, you will see what you did to put you in the situation you're in today. Conversely, when you begin building your future today, you will have a positive effect on how you'll be able to live five years from now.

YOU NEED AN EMPLOYEE

Whatever job you may have, if someone else is signing your paycheck, your income is determined by what you can earn *for them!* If they pay you one dollar, they may hope to make two. That's business. If you own your own business, you probably pay yourself at a level such that the business still stays profitable. You're working for someone or something, whether you're an employer or an employee. It's time to turn the tables.

Whether you have a business or work for someone else, you're looking to make money for your efforts. You can claim to do it for the satisfaction or for reasons other than money, but let me ask you this: Would you do it for free? Probably not. And it may not be smart to do so. You need to earn something, either now or down the road, for everything you do. Now ask yourself this: Are you making what you're worth? Most people aren't! How about you?

As long as something or someone is controlling your income, it will be difficult to break free of the money mentality and begin living finance. But what if you had an employee who worked for you and earned you money—even while you slept? That could catapult you towards true financial freedom.

The employee you want must be willing to work all hours of the day and night, weekends and holidays too. No strikes, no sick days, no vacation; just working to earn you money. When you find that employee, you'll be able to participate in finance. Once that employee starts working for you, he'll never quit. He'll even attract others to do the same thing.

When you set up your *Future Growth* account, you are *hiring money* to go to work for you, but not like in the other accounts where it sits there and earns interest. In this account your money goes beyond that and is looking to make a return. This account is for investments.

WHY MANY INVESTMENTS DON'T WORK

Some of you may have made investments in the past, perhaps in stocks, bonds, real estate, or other things of value. But maybe they just didn't get you where you wanted to go. In fact you no longer believe there are good investments for average people. You're right!

The reason investments don't work for average people is that *average* people can't leave the money there long enough. Something always comes up where they need to sell the investment. Or perhaps they put all they have into one investment, and when it begins to go down in value, they panic and sell. Inevitably, the investment goes up right after they sell it.

They never really let go of their money long enough to get any quality work out of it. They are so dependent on the money, rather than the other way around, that the money never really has a chance to reach its full potential.

Add this to your affirmation list: *I always make good investments and let my money work to its full potential.*

The key word in that affirmation is *let*. You must be willing to let the money do what it does best—increase in value. There will be fluctuations along the way, but don't let them bother you. Historically, long-term investments have ended on the upside.

HOW MUCH DO YOU NEED TO HAVE TO INVEST?

You may be thinking that since you're just starting out, you don't have huge sums of money to invest. While you may not be able to buy enough stock to own a company, don't think you can't enter the investment game. Having large sums of money does allow certain benefits that may not be available to you right now, but remember that dealing in finance is first a state of mind, then a reality. Once you see that any amount of money can work for you, you're involved in finance.

Let's say you want to become involved with a safe mutual fund. The minimum amount needed is $1,000 to open the account. You decide to set a goal for getting in once you have the $1,000 saved. How often have you done that in your life? How many times have you been successful at it? What if you created investments that had your money working for you right away, and once those investments reached $1,000 you could then switch them to a mutual fund?

When you have all of your accounts set up, you find that you're able to contribute $20 a month into the Future Growth account. Simple math says that in four years and two months you'll have enough to begin participating in the fund. Fifty months from now you can be involved in finance. Too long to wait? Let's get started today.

First of all, even if it took you four years and two months to do this—so what! With what you did over the last four years, are you as well off? And that's if you took a $20 bill and stuck it in the drawer every month for four years! Suppose you put this money to work immediately? Then what would happen?

Well for one thing, it would take less time. In fact, if you earned a meager 2 percent a year on your money, it would take you two months less and you'd have $14.28 extra. Or if you invested at that 2 percent rate for the entire 50 months, you'd have $54.37 extra. Now that may not be a fortune, but it didn't require any extra effort on your part to get it, either. In fact the money did it all without any guidance from you. This is finance. If you were able to get your money earning 4 percent, you would have ended up with over $100 more than you actually put in during the same period. At 8 percent you would have over $200—all without one ounce of extra work on your part.

That's just the beginning. But it's a great example of how finance gets your money to work for you. Once you have a set amount to enter the investment arena, things change. For one thing, your money is going to work harder and provide better income for you.

A POWERFUL MONEY RULE

Einstein once said it was the Eighth Wonder of the World—compound interest. Compounding is what happens as interest is earned on your money. When interest compounds, it basically means that you are earning money not only on your initial investment but *also* on the interest earned on the initial investment.

Here's a simple example. If you had $100 and earned 10 percent interest a year, how much would you earn in one year? You'd earn $10. Now how much would you earn in ten years? Some of you may just multiply the $10 times the ten years and say $100, which would mean you've doubled your money. Not bad—but not right.

In the first year you would earn $10. That means you now have a balance of $110 in your investment account. That balance will now earn 10 percent, and at the end of the second year you will have earned $11, for a total of $121. That occurs because you also earn 10 percent on the $10 interest you received in the first year. At the end of the third year you would have $132.10. After four years, $145.31; five years, $159.84; six, $175.82; seven, $193.40; eight, $212.74; nine, $234.01. And after 10 years you would have $257.41—well *over* twice as much as you started with!

What compounding did for you was double your money somewhere between seven and eight years, not the ten years you may have predicted. With compounding you earned an extra $57.41 over the same period without compounding.

There is a rule that can help you figure this process out. It's called the "Rule of 72." To use this rule you simply divide the interest rate you'll earn into the number 72. The answer will tell you how many years it will take for your money to double. If you can earn 6 percent, it will take 12 years to double your money. If you can earn 8 percent, you double your investment in nine years.

As your accounts grow, you'll be able to move your money into other areas that could earn even more for you. While this book isn't meant to teach you about investments, you should know that if you were able to find some investments that earned 12 percent, you would double your money every six years. Think about how powerful that would be when you're planning your financial future. To put it into perspective, if you were 30 years old and had enough money to invest and earn an average of 12 percent, what would the future hold? Because of the rule of 72, if you invested nothing else, your money would double five times before you turned 60 years old.

That means that $1,000 put into the account today and left there for 30 years would equal $32,000. To understand how powerful that is, realize that you didn't have to put another penny into the account after the initial deposit. That's what I mean by having money work for you.

Why is that important? If you live with money and money problems, it isn't important. But for those of you willing to make the change to finance, it's critical. People who live with a paycheck mentality may not want to go to all the trouble of moving their investment in order to go from earning 6 percent to earning 7 percent. But when you're involved in finance, that could mean earlier retirement. Here's why. As I showed before, at 6 percent you would double your money in twelve years, which isn't bad. If you shifted it to an account or program that earned 7 percent—only 1 percent more—you would double your money in just over ten years! You could retire almost two years earlier! What's two more years of freedom worth to you?

WORRY-FREE INVESTING

The beauty of setting up a Future Growth account is the ability to invest without any pressure. Using the multiple account principle allows you to invest this money without sacrificing your lifestyle or any of the other future programs you are setting up. You can take bigger risks without worrying about losing other assets.

That allows you to think with a clearer head about where you put your money. There are many books and professionals who can advise you as to specific investments, and I suggest you seek them out. You have a big advantage over other investors who are counting on their investments for specifics in their current and future lifestyle. Your lifestyle is being maintained and looked after in the future by the other accounts. This account is strictly for investing. Your investments will simply enhance your future.

You can set time limits that are reasonable for your money, rather than watch it every day, worrying about whether it's up or down. You won't get caught in a panic selling situation. You won't have to sell your investments before they earn their potential because of an emergency somewhere else in your life. The beauty of this account is that you'll send the money out to earn for you, and you don't have to take it back out until it has accomplished its mission.

Debt as a percentage of people's incomes has indeed been rising. In 2000, the average person seeking help had a gross income of $29,738 and a debt load of $26,337—almost 89% of their total income. In 1995 the average member's debt load was around 71% of their income.

National Foundation of Credit Counseling

CHAPTER ELEVEN

The Income
Security Account

*Our problems are man-made; therefore they may
be solved by men. And man can be as big as he
wants. No problem of human destiny is beyond
human beings.*

John F. Kennedy

FACT-OF-LIFE FINANCING

Today's college graduates are being told that they will have
more than 10 jobs and three career changes in their lifetimes.
However, what we may be teaching them is already happening
to us on a fairly consistent basis. While we are teaching our
youth that there is no longer a stigma attached to changing jobs,
over 400,000 people will be laid off from their jobs this year.
Odds are very good that you know someone who has been affected by a sudden change in employment.

What if that someone was you? Are you prepared to bear
your financial responsibilities in the event that the paycheck
you've come to count on suddenly disappears? If you're starting
to feel a bit uneasy as you think about this possibility, keep in
mind, you're not alone. In fact, the majority of those working
today are less than 90 days away from severe financial hardship
if there was an interruption in their income.

This probably isn't the first time that you've heard about
setting up some amount of money for emergencies. Most often,

people are told to put aside three months' worth of income. By the same token, very few people ever get to do it. The reason they don't is because of the "emergencies" that seem to pop up every month—their bills.

Rather than put you under pressure to come up with 90 days of income when you're just beginning to discover the power of finance, let's put this *Income Security* account together over time. This way, you'll eventually get the amount you need to protect yourself in the event of any emergency. Each month you'll be closer to having security than you were the month before.

Once you've achieved whatever that amount is for you, what kind of relief do you suppose you'll feel? Imagine not having to panic if something happens to stop your income. How would it feel to know that, if you should lose your source of income, you won't have to worry about money while you search for a new job opportunity?

Finally, why limit the security to only 90 days? What makes three months the magic number? What if you kept the account active and growing for an even longer form of protection? Imagine having enough in the account to handle a loss of income for an entire year. Better still, what would it feel like to know that if you decided not to go to work for a while, you would have your current level of income available for an entire year?

A REAL PAID VACATION

For many people this is a favorite account. Accomplishing this one means you would be able to take a full year off work without worrying about where the money's coming from. It's different from the Permanent Wealth account in that this one could be used to fund a year off.

As you build this account, you will be getting closer to what many people in finance call *critical mass*. Critical mass occurs when you are able to do the things you've always wanted without sacrificing your future lifestyle. In fact, your finances will continue to grow and expand even when you stop putting money in!

When you reach the point in this account where you have one year's salary, you may want to take the year off. As you read further in this chapter, you will see that this could become an incredible time in your life. But imagine, for now, being able to do what you want for an entire year and *still have the same income coming in*.

The side benefits are incredible.

Suppose you were starting to be pressured at work. How you handled it would determine your immediate future with your job. If you had been building the Income Security account for a while, how much could what happens at work *really* bother you? While others may react in a negative fashion, you are positive and able to continue as if nothing had happened. Your supervisors, upon seeing your attitude, may recommend you for a promotion, raise, or some other reward.

On the other hand, if it got to be too negative an environment, you would have options. Others who had not been preparing would have to take what they were dealt and live with it. You could afford to leave if you have the whole year taken care of or, if not, at least take time off to look for another job, or start a business, without worrying about your obligations.

WHAT ABOUT ALONG THE WAY?

Earlier I mentioned the importance of rewarding yourself along the way with small incentives. Since for many people this will not be one of the faster growing accounts, those rewards will be key in keeping you going. The incentives here need to be both physical and mental. You need the actual reward in your hand, as well as the strengthening of your mind, to keep going.

To help you see this, I am going to use simple numbers for ease of explanation. I am going to use an annual income of $36,500. For some of you that may be more than you are earning; for others, less. I chose this number because it breaks down to $100 a day. While $36,500 may be hard to imagine, most of us can picture $100 a day.

The first reward you should take is when you have one week's pay in the account. When that happens, take a day off. The night before, put $100 in an envelope, mark it "PAY," and place it where you'll see it when you wake up. That morning you can go anywhere and do anything, knowing that you've already been paid.

Once you've saved an entire month's income ($3,100), reward yourself with a week off. You will really begin feeling what it's like to be totally independent of work because you will have seven envelopes, each with $100 in them. You don't need to worry about getting back on the job because you've taken care of insuring your future income.

Each time you reward yourself you will notice the payback is larger. The purpose here is to give you more incentive to keep going and doing it as quickly as possible. As you reach a level of three months, you might consider taking an entire month off. Whether you do or you don't isn't as important as knowing that *you could*. That gives you control.

FOLLOW YOUR DREAM—THE MONEY WILL COME

Here's what could happen when you achieve your goal of a year's income in savings. While this is an individual example and certainly not guaranteed, I believe it isn't really that rare a possibility.

This person was in sales for many years and was quite successful at it. If you saw all the trappings of success, you'd agree. Unfortunately, he could keep those trappings only if he continued to earn his high income. His debt load was eating up over half his annual salary. He looked at other ways of increasing his income without jeopardizing his *status*.

He began to realize that in order to get ahead, he would need to put in more work and more hours. This meant less time to enjoy all the *things* he had purchased for enjoyment.

On top of that, his family was becoming more distant. He was spending more time away from them, trying to give them the creature comforts he thought they wanted. What they really wanted was him!

Someone he knew from work asked him to look at a business that he was starting near where they both lived. It was based internationally but had local operations everywhere. The benefits of the business were great, and he decided to give it a serious look.

Everyone seemed to make fun of him. They asked why someone so successful would need a side job to make ends meet. Fortunately, he looked at the merits of the opportunity and his strong desire to eliminate debt and decided that this was for him.

As with most businesses, it was difficult in the beginning. He understood that like all investments, this would pay off over time. Using his free time today was an investment in *time freedom* in the future. In fact, it took almost all his free time and effort just to get it moving. But once it started, even he couldn't stop it. Because he worked so hard in the beginning and put his focus on accomplishing his goals, the business grew to the point where he could decide whether he wanted to continue working at his regular job.

YOU CAN DO IT SOONER THAN YOU THINK

You may be thinking about how impossible it is to save an entire year's salary. That feeling is probably based on the fact that you've never done it before, so why should you be able to do it now? First and foremost, believe it can be done. Nature taught me that things always grow from the inside out, and so it is with success and wealth. *Things don't just "turn up;" success comes from people turning things up*.

Another thing that may encourage you is that I don't believe you need to save that entire salary to have enough for a year off. You're reading this book because you're in debt and as such, part of your yearly salary is going towards monthly payment of that debt. If we used the $36,500 example again and also used the national average debt of $19,000 (not counting the mortgage), how much would you need if you were debt-free?

A lot depends on what you owed the $19,000 on. Let's assume that $10,000 is on a car loan, and the other $9,000 is in credit card debt of $3,000 on each of three cards. We'll say the monthly car payment is $300 and the credit cards require a minimum of $100 each. We'll also assume a mortgage payment of $1,000 a month. That means $1,600 of your monthly income is going towards payments, for a total of $19,200 a year for debt. That means if you didn't owe any money, you would only need $17,300 to live exactly as you've been living on $36,500.

Now $17,300 is still a large number, but if you were debt-free and still earning $36,500, how fast could you save it? Well, regardless of how much you had been saving up until the point when you became debt-free, you could now add an additional $19,200 a year to the account. In fact, even at a low interest rate, if you began saving the day you became debt-free, it would take you less than two years to have enough money to take a year off!

THE PAST DOES NOT EQUAL THE FUTURE

I can understand that having a whole year's salary in the bank is hard to imagine. It's probably even harder when it's only *one* of your accounts. But think about how much money has passed through your fingers since you began working. If the money hadn't gotten away due to debt, caused by buying things now instead of saving for them and by simple lack of planning, isn't it possible that you could have had that money in the bank right now?

Just because what you did in the past may have prevented you from being able to take a year off today, doesn't mean you can't begin a plan to take a year off in the future. What you did in the past is done. Use it as a lesson and not an excuse. Don't let mistakes of the past become habits for the future.

The only thing I am fairly certain about in the near future is that it will happen. In five years you will be five years older. The choice you need to make is, will you be closer to being able to take a year off, or will things have remained as they are?

It's not about money. It's about control. Whether you have debt or not has nothing to do with your income. With debt you lose control of where your money goes—you no longer decide the best way to spend the money you've worked for.

John Fuhrman

CHAPTER TWELVE

The Debt Elimination Account

He is strong who conquers others; he who conquers himself is mighty.

Lao Tzu

CHAINS THAT BIND

When you have a bad day at work, what can you do about it? Chances are, not much more than either keep it inside or take it out on friends and family. Ninety-six percent of the population will not reach financial independence in their lifetime. Most of them are underpaid or totally dissatisfied with their jobs. Seventy percent of the people hate to go to work.

Everyone should be able to live their dreams. The quality of life would vastly improve, and a lot of social problems would vanish. That's such a great idea, yet why do most people live lives of quiet desperation? The reason is many people *can't* follow their dreams. The problem is debt. If you owe as much as the average individual, you are often forced to do the kind of work that gives you enough income to keep your head above water. Why not just work where you can earn more money for the same job?

What determines your pay? It used to be things like ability, seniority, geographic area, and other outside factors. Today your pay is determined by the demand of the job and the cost to replace you. Think about it. If 96 percent of the workforce are in debt, and they're looking to keep their heads above water, how much of a threat would it be for you to tell your boss to pay more or you'd leave? In other words, if you left, how quickly could you be replaced with someone else who has *obligations?*

YOUR ONLY TEMPORARY ACCOUNT

Setting up an account whose sole purpose is to eliminate debt can be a great relief as soon as you open it. The very moment you make the first deposit, you will have taken a bigger step toward freedom from money than with all the other accounts put together. This high-powered account will end up giving you more control over your life than all the others combined.

Once it does that, you close it out. This account is like a high-priced consultant that solves a company's problems, collects a high fee, and vanishes. You will use every ounce of this account's ability to work for you, and then you can fire it. No hard feelings. When it's time for this account to be closed, you will be so close to financial freedom, you can taste it.

The other great thing that happens when this account is gone is the increase in growth in all the others. When you no longer need this account, your financial wealth grows at an increased rate. This increase is even more freeing because, having eliminated all your debt, you need even less to live the way you want. But if your income continues at its present level, you will save at an even greater rate.

THE SETUP

Once you decide how much of your money will go into this account, you need to decide how often to use it. This is important because eliminating debt can get discouraging. If you don't use the account often enough, it appears as if nothing is happening. If you use it too often, there might not be enough money in it to make a significant difference.

Keep in mind that this is only *one* of your accounts. Many people who tried to eliminate debt before did it by putting all their extra money towards bills. They didn't build other areas of financial purpose. The result of all that effort was that, just like after any difficult task, they were drained. By having these other accounts working for you, you'll find it easier to become more encouraged with every step.

I recommend using whatever is in the account every 90 days. The time frame is not too long or too short, and you have three months of deposits to work with. While it probably won't amount to thousands in the beginning, you will see that as you eliminate debts, this account will grow bigger and become more powerful.

START SMALL

List all of your obligations on a sheet of paper. If this is the first time you've done this, you may be amazed at how much debt you have. Or you may be surprised that you're not as far in debt as you thought. Either way, having no debt is the only objective, and this method will help you pay all of it in a shorter time than you can imagine.

Now that you have your list, you need to put it in order. The first time you sort them, list them from smallest to largest; if you have a mortgage, it would probably be last. Then take the ones with similar balances and sort them by interest rate, listing the higher rate first. For example, if you have two debts of approximately $400 each, and one is to the dentist and the other is to a credit card company at 18 percent interest, the credit card should be listed first. Rank all debts this way.

The reason you need to do this is because the higher rates are the ones eating up your monthly payment and reducing what you owe by only crumbs. You want to attack those high-rate debts with extra principal (the real amount you owe) payments to reduce and quickly eliminate your debt.

As soon as you eliminate a debt, your *Debt Elimination* account becomes more powerful. First, the power increases because you saw it in action. You proved it could be done. That will give you the encouragement to go after a larger account without fear. The second power source is the increase you can now put into the account.

Let's say that a $400 debt was costing you $30 a month. Each month you paid $30 toward this debt, and every 90 days you would reduce the principal by whatever you had in your Debt Elimination account. Suppose you started by designating $15 a month to this account. That would mean that every 90 days, an additional $45 would go to reducing debt. Doing that, you would be able to pay off this $400 obligation in less than nine months.

Once that debt is eliminated, what will you do with the freed-up $30 a month that you no longer owe?

The beauty of this entire program is its flexibility. You can do whatever you like. Since we've discussed six accounts, you can put $5 in each, $10 in your favorite three, or all $30 into your Debt Elimination account. What would that do?

Let's say the next bill on the list is $1,500. The minimum payment is $50, and it would take six more years to pay it off using the minimum. By putting the entire $30 from your paid-off debt of $400 into the account, you would have an extra $90 every three months. Every 90 days you would be able to make a payment of the $50 you paid every month, the $45 you had been putting into the account from the beginning, and the extra $90 you now had available from your newly retired debt of $400. That means that every 90 days you could make a payment of $185, of which at least $135 goes entirely to principal! You would eliminate that debt in less than two years. That's four years early!

IT KEEPS GETTING BETTER

Estimates say that 85 percent of car owners have financed their transportation, many of them for five years (banks will now lend for up to seven years!). The average new car payment is just under $400 a month, based on an average loan of around $24,000. For this example, let's assume you're average, and to keep it simple, assume you just bought this car. How quickly can you eliminate this five-year debt?

Let's add it up. You are no longer paying on your two smaller loans ($30 and $50 a month). You are still saving $45 every three months. Totaling these deposits equals $285 every 90 days. Keep in mind, you haven't changed anything you've been doing. You just keep depositing your $45 and *make the other monthly payments to yourself*. The result is you would own your car in roughly four years.

What happens now?

Let's see where you'll be 12 months later. Now, instead of paying the financial institution, you can put your former car payments into the bank. This, along with your other payments, and the $45 you save every quarter, would give you a grand total of over $8,000! All that money, without changing your lifestyle one bit. And that's assuming you never get a pay raise or earn any interest on the money you deposit.

You have your vehicle and $8,000 to look for a nice car. Next time however, buy one that's three or four years old. It'll only cost about half what a new one does and still look and drive great. Take advantage of the depreciation somebody else paid for. New car debt is probably the biggest wealth-stealer there is.

Now we'll assume that you use your car for three years after it's paid off, before you want to trade it in. (Incidentally, the average car on the road is eight years old.) By then you would have put aside over $16,000 plus interest, *plus you have a car that you own free and clear!* Who do you suppose gets the best deal now—you or the bank?

Another option is if you have a mortgage. Instead of paying

through the nose for a new car, you can apply the payments that you would have been making, which now total almost $1,500 every 90 days, to your existing mortgage! That would save tens of thousands of dollars and literally years off the term of your mortgage! What kind of freedom would you have with no mortgage? How would that make you feel?

WORKING WITH FINANCE

Everything you just read is not only possible but simple. If you followed these examples, understand that you never changed your current lifestyle. You did all of this with the money you were already spending and the $45 you saved every three months. You didn't have to search for more money or sacrifice the way you were living. You simply needed to learn where your money was going, not add any more debts, pay off one debt, and then redirect the freed-up cash towards another.

When you do that, you change from being a slave to being the master of your money. You don't have to wait until you're debt-free to master money. In fact, the day you decide to put this program into action, you switch your mentality from working for money to having money work for you. You go from paycheck mentality to wealth mentality.

DON'T YOU NEED CREDIT CARDS TO LIVE TODAY?

If you want to rent a car, they ask for a credit card. Check into a hotel, they want an imprint of a major credit card. Business lunches and the like use credit cards as a way of providing records for tax purposes. And if you have a credit card, no real discipline, and see the bargain of a lifetime . . . Well, you probably know what'll happen.

The realities of the world today are such that you need some kind of credit card to do any kind of travel or business. Having one certainly eliminates the potential hazard of carrying large amounts of cash on trips, as well as providing a form of identification for rental cars, hotels, and the like. There are two options that I recommend.

The simplest one is to check with your local bank. Many banks today are using one of the major credit card companies on their ATM cards. That means when you use them in a restaurant, the charges are immediately deducted from your bank account. It looks like and acts like and is accepted like a major credit card. The only difference is there is never a monthly balance or interest fee.

The second choice is the type of credit card called an "entertainment card." These cards (American Express, Diners Club) were named this for the simple reason that they were initially used as a record keeping tool for business people to track their expenses. This type of card also does not generally allow you to carry a balance, so all charges are paid monthly. Be careful though. Unlike your bankcard, these cards generally let you keep on charging throughout the month. They don't call you when your account gets too low on funds. You could find you need to come up with money that you don't have.

Another caution with these cards is the different levels available. You should never need more than the basic services they provide. Forget the difference between the status of a gold or platinum as opposed to a lowly green card. You can do just fine by using the green to hold onto your green (cash). The fees of these cards range from $50 a year for basic (again, this is all you need) to $300 for the executive type card. Shop around. Sometimes these cards are offered for no fee. Just remember, the color of your card has no bearing on your success.

LET'S RECYCLE

You've already read that this account is only temporary. You can just toss it aside as soon as you're out of debt. But with all the talk in the world today about conservation, what about recycling this account?

If you choose to continue using this account, you can call it whatever you like. You can also allocate funds any way that you like. It could be the *New Car* account, or *Disney World For a Week* account, or even *College for the Kids* account. It can be whatever you like. You already know it'll work for you in whatever way you choose, so why not?

Using the figures from the earlier example, you'd have $1,500 every three months. You could begin this new account with the $15 per month that was going to the Debt Elimination account, which is $45 every three months. That leaves $1,455 every 90 days, or $485 a month, to be split into what now amounts to seven accounts. You'll be able to add an extra $69 and change to each account every month.

If you have one account that you are more partial to, you can shift this money any way you wish without changing what you're already contributing to the other accounts. That's the beauty of being debt-free—the first and perhaps most important step toward total financial freedom.

PART THREE

POWERFUL CHANGES

Most Americans are less than 90 days away from bankruptcy should their income be interrupted due to illness, loss of job, or other emergency.

Unknown

CHAPTER THIRTEEN

Start Small

What saves a man is to take a step. Then another step.

Antoine de Saint-Exupery

YOU CAN'T GET RICH WITHOUT IT

When people consider doing something to get out of debt and dream of financial freedom, many of them imagine a huge sum of money as the answer. They often think of a million dollars or more as the magic figure. The challenge with that type of thinking is that most people aren't able to relate to a million or more of anything. I'm an advocate of thinking big, especially since it doesn't require any more energy to do so. However, you need to start small and keep going. Success in anything is made up of a series of baby steps.

If you are in debt, it may be a stretch, especially at first, to imagine having a million dollars. Couple that with the fact that you're at your current income level based on what you're now doing, and it may be challenging for your mind to imagine where the extra money will come from. This is where your logical side takes over. It may try to convince you to settle for what you have, because mathematically, based on what you now do for a living, it may seem impossible to save one million dollars. So what do you do?

You need to change your thinking. Your current thought patterns aren't supporting you in achieving financial freedom because you're thinking of starting at the end—when you have

109

the million! Your logical mind sees this as impossible, but it's not—it's essential. You must, as Stephen Covey says in his best-selling book *The Seven Habits of Highly Effective People*, "Begin with the end in mind." Covey explains, ". . . (this) means to start with a clear understanding of your destination. . . . to know where you're going so you better understand where you are now and so the steps you take are always in the right direction."

Your logical mind sees a million dollars and it sees your annual income. In all likelihood, they don't add up. What logic can't see is the in-between steps. Let's look at an example to help you retrain your logical mind.

Suppose you earn $40,000 per year. (If you live outside the United States, figure this using the dollar equivalency.) Say you have mortgage payments of $1,000 a month, other debt of $1,000 a month, and the day-to-day living expenses we all have. If you pay 25 percent of your total income to taxes, that leaves you with a net income of $30,000 a year. Subtract your debt, and you are left with $6,000 for food, clothing, and other items. Now say you could get by on only $5,000 of what's left for the remaining expenses. That would leave you with a surplus of $1,000 a year.

In order to save $1,000,000, at $1,000 a year, it would take hundreds of years, even if you were earning a large return on your money. Your logical mind can see this, understands you won't live that long, computes it all, and, in all likelihood, tells you to settle for the long road of mediocrity. However, it left out one key element—eliminating debt! What if you had no debt? Then how long would it take?

Well, based on the above example, without debt, you'd be able to save $25,000 ($30,000 net income minus $5,000 in expenses) without changing your current lifestyle. Investing that $25,000 every year at a compound interest rate of 10 percent would give you over a million dollars in 17 years. Investing it at 12 percent compounded would give you a million in only 15$\frac{1}{2}$ years! That's not very long compared to several centuries. No wonder, if you have debt, your logical side would discourage you. But even debt is still not the most important element.

Start saving! It doesn't matter how much—just start getting in *the habit*! Even if you wanted to save only $100, you wouldn't generally start with $99. Put aside what you can and *leave it there*. As it builds, through your regular contributions and the interest that it earns, you're taking steps toward your dream. In the previous example, $1,000,000 is the destination and each deposit is a step towards it. At first it may appear to be a slow, seemingly never-ending journey. Remember, one of the keys to success is *persistence*! Later I'll be sharing a way for you to get there more quickly and to have fun while you're doing it!

A CHANGE WITH CHANGE

For a long time, I had an attitude about saving that certainly didn't support ever getting out of debt and becoming financially free. As my family and my obligations grew, I became more convinced that my attitude was right. Whenever the subject of saving money came up, I'd respond by saying that I'll begin to save as soon as I have enough money. Think about that. Have you ever said the same thing?

If you never start saving, how will you ever have enough to start? The amount you're saving at first isn't as important as the necessary *steps* to begin your savings program. I learned that when my wife was cleaning up my usually messy office.

She was simply putting things away when she noticed loose change (coins) everywhere. I don't like carrying change around with me, so I frequently empty my pockets wherever I am in the house. So Helen went and got an old mayonnaise jar and began putting my change in it. After about a month, I was amazed at how much change I had unthinkingly left around.

I took the jar of money to my bank, where they have a coin-counting machine. The teller emptied the jar and came back a few minutes later. She handed me a slip with $38 written on it! The teller then asked me what I'd like to do with the money—deposit it or take the cash. I suddenly realized that the time to save was now! I had casually disregarded the importance of this money. It just never seemed like much—not enough to bother with. But the fact is, I had money all along that I could have been saving and earning compounded interest on. How encouraging this realization was!

Think about it. Since I had left $38 around the house without even missing it, couldn't I start saving at least that much? At that point I decided to *start thinking* about where my money goes. Before I began saving, I was holding myself back by the idea that I needed to start with at least $50 a month. Before, when the end of each month came and I didn't have the *extra* $50, I quit my savings program. But there really wasn't anything to quit since I had never even taken the first step!

Once I realized that I only needed to come up with an additional $12 to add to the change I was throwing around the house—to have the $50—the rest suddenly became easy. I then realized that I could at least begin building a future of financial freedom. How about you? Are you really as far away from beginning a savings program as you once thought? And if you haven't moved on it yet, the time to get started is *now*! As the old saying goes, "There's no time like the present."

HABITS THAT MAKE YOU GROW

As the months went by and our little $50-a-month savings account began to grow, consistently putting the money in our account became a *new habit*. In fact, we didn't even miss the money! However, even though we were persistently saving our $50 each month, our old habits that caused the money pressures in the first place were still there.

Savings are only a small part of the picture of achieving financial freedom, although it's an important place to start. It's likely you'll need to change at least some of your spending habits as well as the size of your debt load. Here's how I began to add the new wealth-inducing habits so I could grow towards the financial freedom I wanted for myself and my family.

The first thing I realized was that my new success with saving money came about because, even though I began small, at least I *started saving something* each month. And similarly, since I wanted to wipe out our debts, I needed, above all else, to *get started*. The monthly amount wasn't as important as the fact that I was developing a new habit. It became apparent that, as Booker T. Washington once said, "Any man's life will be filled with constant and unexpected encouragement if he makes up his mind to do his level best each day." Doing my best in this area meant that *I needed to replace my old in-debt financial habits with new wealth-oriented ones*. This is what most people fail to do and why their efforts don't lead to the results they claim they want.

One question I had, and you may have it too, was, "What good are savings if I owe people more than I have saved?" I didn't want to part with the money I had saved so far. However, from that point on, I decided to put half of my monthly savings toward the debts that were hanging over us.

When I began applying the $25 each month toward debt elimination, two amazing things took place that totally changed our lives. First, I became very disappointed at how the growth of our savings account had slowed down. I actually began missing the $25 that was now going toward our debts! I then became motivated to *save even more* because our savings, due to decreased compounding of interest, were now increasing more slowly than before. With my new savings habit, I had a created a *new expectation* of our ability to save each month. I had also gotten quite used to our money compounding at a faster rate. So, *we simply needed to find a way* to replace that $25 and get back to growing our savings at the rate that was already a solid new habit.

At the same time, I was beginning to feel excited at how much more quickly our debts were being reduced. Most debts are calculated at simple interest. That means the interest or finance charges are calculated on the unpaid balance. When you pay money in addition to your regular monthly payment amount, it's applied directly to the principal balance. This means the entire $25 went right toward the amount I owed.

This excited me so much that I wanted to find some more money to make the debts disappear even faster!

In the next chapter, I'll share where we found some of this extra money. You will see easy ways to pick up a little bit here and a little bit there. When you apply some of it to debt and some of it to savings, things really began to happen.

CHAPTER FOURTEEN

Creating Wealth

Man's mind once stretched by a new idea, never regains its original dimension.

Oliver Wendall Holmes

DIGGING FOR WEALTH AT HOME

Did you ever have a project to do around the house and you needed a specific tool? You're positive you have it but you can't find it. The harder you look, the less sure you are that you have it. You finally give up, go to the hardware store and buy it. No sooner do you arrive at home that you realize where it was all along.

Wealth is the same way. Many have spent lifetimes looking for fortunes in faraway lands, only to miss what was right under their noses. I'm not trying to tell you that everyone has the secret to wealth right in their own home, but the seeds to growing a secure future are most certainly there. We need to look with the eyes of an explorer who wants to make a fantastic discovery. If you simply scan the room, you may miss it. However, those who are willing to crawl around and look in every nook and cranny will find seeds that will grow.

If you own your home, you have a veritable money machine if you handle it properly. This doesn't require piles of money poured into additions or swimming pools and the like. If something breaks, leaks, or needs fixing, repair it right away. Not only will this generally prevent further expensive damage, but it will also maintain and perhaps increase the value of your home.

Once we had a very slight leak in a shower drainpipe. It was so slight that in a week of constant use, less than a half-inch of water accumulated in a bucket. I replaced the pipe, which was plastic, for around $10, and it hasn't leaked since. Had I ignored the leak, which dripped into the basement, here's what could have happened. The constant dampness could have created a mold situation in the laundry room. In addition, it could have splashed onto the wall and eventually softened it up to where it had to be repaired. In other words, a $10 repair could have easily become $100 or more.

Now for some of you $100 may not be a fortune, but think of it in terms of finance. By investing your $10 immediately in the repair, you would in effect have a 1,000 percent return on that investment! Once you have that kind of return on investment, you can grow wealth very quickly.

In making major household purchases, buy quality instead of price. If you could buy an appliance for $200 that will last four years, or spend $300 for one that lasts eight, which do you buy? While one seems to save you $100 today, over the life of the appliances, the more expensive one will save you $100. And that's if prices don't rise over the eight years. In finance terms, you will save a minimum of 33 percent plus interest if the prices never change.

On anything major concerning your house, picture yourself selling it tomorrow. Imagine having to put your house up for sale as soon as whatever you want to do is done, and ask yourself, "Will I be able to recover this money in the sale price?" If it is a needed repair, that's different. You may not be able to calculate the price of the job, but you probably couldn't sell the house until it was done. However, if you were considering an addition that made your house much bigger and more expensive than any other in the neighborhood, you may not be able to get much of it back.

USE YOUR IMAGINATION

Did you ever want something just for yourself? Since it wasn't something for the entire family, did you put off getting it because you didn't want to take family money to buy it? That happened to me. Years ago, I wanted a metal detector. I don't remember why I wanted it but I did. The one I wanted was about $400. I didn't dare take from the family funds to get it, especially since I could only use it once in a great while. It was truly a frivolous *toy* for me. Where would I get the money?

As I was deciding which one to get, I read many magazines on the subject. One of them advertised for articles that they would pay for. I made an agreement with my wife. I would write these articles before everyone got up and after everyone went to bed. I would still participate in all family activities and do what needed doing around the house. Then, if I made enough money from these articles, I could buy the detector. I wrote four pieces for two different magazines and made enough money for the purchase.

As a bonus, once I had the detector and learned how to use it, I was able to do another story on some discoveries and had it published too. So by using my imagination, I was not only able to achieve my objective and get the detector, but I was able to use my new purchase to earn even more. My thinking created profits.

Let your own creativity help you. Allow it to become a wealth-building tool. Use it before you see if there's enough money in the account to cover a purchase. Better still, imagine ways to come up with money to eliminate a debt.

Suppose you owed $1,000 on a credit card. While setting up your accounts as we've discussed will help eliminate debt faster than other methods, what if you used some of your own creativity? Clear your mind and think of a deadline. You need to come up with $1,000 in 30 days. How will you do it? The first time you try this, you may not get so much as a passing thought. Don't give up. Like any exercise, you get better and the exercise becomes more effective as you continue.

Each day when you wake up, write down three solutions to eliminate a debt. Many of them will be pretty far-fetched but that's okay. Continue doing this every day. Settle for nothing less than three ideas. An amazing thing will happen. If you do this consistently, one idea will keep popping up. This idea will take on a life of its own. What that means is it will fill in its own blanks, giving you details on exactly how to achieve what the idea tells you.

As with anything new, start small. Work on getting the process correct. Stay simple until you have comfortably formed the habit of writing down three profitable ideas a day. Remember, everything grows from the inside out. These ideas are nothing more than seeds you toss out onto the soil. Some will never do anything. Others will sprout with potential and then wither and die. A few will grow with strong roots and flourish. These will take the longest—but they will be the only ones that produce fruit. Wait for them to get ripe before you pick them, and the sweetness will be your reward.

REMEMBER BEFORE YOU ACT

Old ideas and habits don't simply go away. In fact, they often create conflict and possibly backsliding into your old ways. New ideas and practices will require effort to help them get a strong hold so they can change your thinking.

> *Never run from something in fear. Rather run*
> *towards something with anticipation.*

When you look back over your shoulder, what's behind you has a better chance of catching up with you. You've taken your eyes off your goal. Should it get too close, some people have a tendency to surrender and return to their old ways. You need to *focus on where you're going with everything you have.* A constant focus will get ever clearer with each step you take.

Instead of putting *only* $10 in the bank and dwelling on the hundreds of dollars you are in debt, look at the deposit as putting you closer to freedom. In fact, you are closer to financial independence than at any other time in your life. That's because up until this very moment, your account had $10 less in it before you made the deposit.

The secret to having a million dollars is a simple one. There is one ingredient that must exist before anyone can ever hope to achieve millionaire status. In order to acquire a million dollars you must have one thing first. You must have that first dollar. You can't start at $999,999 and then hope to earn a dollar. To get to two dollars, you need to get to one first. And I assure you it is much easier to save a dollar when you're starting out than it is to save a hundred when you're trying to catch up.

At age 65, 75% of the population are dependent on relatives or charity, 23% are still working, and 2% are self-sustaining. And 85 out of 100 people reaching the age of 65 do not even have a paltry $250.

Social Security Administration

CHAPTER FIFTEEN

Speeding Up
the Process

*Money doesn't grow on trees; you've got to beat the
bushes for it.*

Unknown

CAN YOU FIND SOME EXTRA MONEY?

Once you get started on the road to financial freedom, you may
want to get there sooner. You'll need to use your powers of creativity to find solutions that create extra money being placed
into your accounts. We'll discuss opportunities to increase your
income in a short while. For those who can't find the time or
take advantage of those opportunities, there are still ways to increase the money going into each account.

Let's start with one avenue that you can use to increase the
amount deposited into your favorite account(s). You decide
how much of this extra money can be placed in any one or all of
the accounts. This is your reward for coming up with creative
ways to get more money working for you.

We'll start with something you spend money on every
single week: food. Each week or so you go shopping for groceries to carry you through until the next time you can get
back to the store. Generally, finding money here is a two-step
process. However, certain rules should apply to every visit to
the supermarket.

First and foremost, you should always have a list for all items that you're going to purchase. If it's not on the list, you can probably get by without it. Second, you should look for sale items for each of your purchases. Finally, everything you buy should be recorded. Fortunately, most stores record the items purchased on your receipt.

The reason this process usually develops over two trips is because the first trip establishes your baseline. In other words, this trip will determine the normal needs for each shopping period. While there may be certain items that aren't purchased on a weekly basis, much of what we live on is bought weekly.

After you've put away all the groceries from this week's shopping trip, have a seat and review your receipt. First make certain that you bought only items that you truly need to have. Then take a moment to clear your mind. Now ask yourself this question: "How can I eat and live as well for 10 percent less than I spent this week?" Get creative.

If you're spending $100 a week on groceries and reduce the bill by 10 percent and still eat as well as before, you can save over $500 a year. That may be enough to eliminate a small credit card balance. It may mean an extra few dollars into your Totally Fun account. It also shows that you can come up with extra money once you have a reason to get creative.

MAKE THEM EARN YOUR BUSINESS

Which phone company do you use? Who cuts and styles your hair? What does your Internet company cost you each month? Which cable TV package do you have? These questions can provide information, but there is a more powerful one that will provide savings. Ask yourself if any of them are the best deal for you.

Can you get a cheaper long distance service? If yes, how much can you save? Even if it's only $5 a month, that's $60 a year. Going to a franchise as opposed to a high-priced stylist can save you $10, $20, or more every month. And if you shop around, you'll find one that provides you the quality of service you're entitled to. Plus you'll save $120 to $240 or more each year.

Local Internet services can be more than half as costly as many of the national ones. Take a hard look at who is providing your service and what you are really using. It's the same thing with your cable company. If you have one of those movie packages and find yourself watching only one movie or so every month, changing to the basic service and renting a movie every now and then can save a bundle.

Making changes in these few areas alone can save you $400 to $600 per year. Couple that with grocery savings and you'll be gaining $1,000 a year to work for you instead of you having to work extra to come up with this money. More importantly, you won't miss any of the things you've given up. That's just another step you're taking toward total control of your financial future.

SOMETHING YOU SHOULD SUBSCRIBE TO

How many magazines do you get every month? What would your life be like without them? What if you spent time reading your favorite magazines at your local library instead of paying for them every year? In addition to saving money, you'd also be occupying some of your free time that may have been used to make spur-of-the-moment purchases in the past.

In a library setting, you'll probably read more of the articles in each magazine than you now do in the comfort of your own home. Bring a notebook and write down any new knowledge you gain from reading those articles. You may find projects to do or day trips that can be taken at no cost to you.

Some of these tips may seem extreme to you. Your individual lifestyle may not be able to handle them all. You may even feel that some of these tips border on becoming miserly. That's okay. I'm not suggesting that you give up everything and spend only on the bare essentials. I'm offering ideas that may help you achieve your goals a bit faster. If these ideas don't appeal to you, perhaps they'll at least get you thinking in new ways about working toward your goals.

WHAT ABOUT INCREASING INCOME?

Another way to eliminate debt and add to your lifestyle is to increase the amount of money passing through your accounts every month. There are many possibilities to accomplish this. Let's explore a few.

Time on the job often leads automatically to increased income. As you stay with your current employer, it is likely that you'll receive periodic raises in salary. Regardless of how slight the increase is, nearly all of it can go toward your future financial goals. While there will be increases in the costs associated with where you live and the services you use, there should always be a portion of your increase that will be left over.

There may be better job opportunities that you can take advantage of. While I'm not suggesting that you start looking to change where you work, it's often true that your increased experience can have a higher value somewhere else. However, I caution you to look at all angles before making any changes. For example, will it cost more to live where the new opportunity is located? Will your expenses go up by more than the increase in salary? You must consider commuting costs, possible childcare issues, and other expenses unique to your situation.

If those are not issues of concern, it is important to look at what this increase in income really can mean for you. You can continue using the same formula you've been using. Taking 10 percent from your new level of income will allow you a bit more freedom to spend and still accelerate your journey to financial freedom. But you can also opt to place all of the increased earnings into your accounts and arrive at your destination even sooner. Neither path is wrong, but you must be the one to choose. As I've shared throughout this book, the key to converting your life from making money to dealing in finance is for you to be in control of where your money goes.

WHAT ELSE CAN YOU DO?

While you may not have considered this, one possibility is to generate some part-time income. Many of you have never considered getting a part-time job before. I can understand that. Those jobs generally don't pay very well and usually there are no benefits. But you're not looking for a career package. You're looking for extra cash.

Keep in mind, this is only short-term. You can set a date that your part-time career would end by calculating when you would achieve financial independence. Obviously, that date will come sooner if you put all of your part-time earnings into your different accounts. However, as long as you're contributing to your future, there is no right or wrong answer.

Calculate what your financial picture would look like with an extra $300 per month going into your accounts. You can use the same percentages that you've been using all along to maintain consistency. Figure out when all of your debts would be paid without the part-time income. Then calculate how much sooner it happens with some extra cash coming in. Now you can intelligently determine whether it's worth it. If you feel you need more money, you can search for a higher-paying part-time job or look for one that provides more hours.

ONE LAST OPTION

There is a trend in America today that is changing the way many people do business. Each year thousands start their own home-based businesses and earn incomes that have opened quite a few eyes. However, even if you earn the same as you would from having a part-time job, you also may be entitled to certain tax benefits.

One home-based business in particular may be more attractive to you. There are many companies with literally thousands of products that participate in this type of business. This kind of business has been around for decades and has proven it-self as something that nearly anyone can do.

The real benefit of this type of business is that if you do it correctly, the income you earn can become residual. What that means is your income can continue long after you stop work-ing. Unlike a regular part-time job, where the pay stops on the day you quit, setting up a residual income allows you to keep earning long after the work is done.

Different companies call it different names, but essentially it's the same process. The most common name for the industry is *network marketing*. While some of you may be sneering at that name because of past experience, I've actually worked with many of the top producers in this industry. Most people are turned off to it because they seem to think it's nothing more than a get-rich-quick scheme. Actually, it's just the opposite.

Those who are earning large incomes have done a lot of hard work over a period of years. I'm not here to suggest that for you. I want to open your eyes to the possibility of generating a few hundred dollars a month to accelerate your journey to-ward financial freedom.

As I said, the unique aspect of network marketing is that once you have developed a foundation that generates the in-come you want, you can often just maintain it and the money keeps on coming in. That's residual income.

A good example of residual income is royalties from an al-bum that musicians record. In many cases they don't earn very much, if any, income while they're in the studio. However, when someone buys their album, even years later, the artist earns a royalty. They do the work today for income in the future. (For more information on network marketing and how it works, visit www.CreditDiet.com.)

USE YOUR IMAGINATION

This chapter offers some alternatives that may help you achieve your goal faster. This is far from a listing of all the possible ways you can generate extra income. Perhaps none of these ideas work for you, but they at least get you to think of other possibilities for saving money. If I've accomplished only that, I've been successful with this chapter.

Finding your financial creativity can motivate you more than any of the previous ideas. Discovering your own ways to generate cash flow and then following through on them will certainly help create a brighter future for you and your family.

Look at things you already enjoy doing and see if there is a way to turn them into income-producing sources. If so, the quality of service you provide will be at a higher level because you already enjoy doing what you do. The only difference is that you have figured out how to get paid for it.

PART FOUR

PRACTICAL ADVICE

Next year is now. Where you end up in the next 365 days will be determined by what you're willing to do today.

John Fuhrman

CHAPTER SIXTEEN

It Has to Be Fun

A happy heart is better than a full purse.

Italian Proverb

A GAME OR ANOTHER JOB?

Beginning on your journey toward financial freedom can create many feelings. For some of you it may bring relief; for others, excitement; and for a few of you, a vision of the hard work and sacrifice you think are required to become debt-free. I caution any of you who feel that way to be careful.

If the going were to get tough, it's possible that you could go through a process called justification. Your reasons for changing your financial destiny become unclear and begin to change. They change from things like security and freedom to materialism and greed. You begin to tell yourself how you've done okay so far and you're not into money, so why do all this?

People will always quit over material things, but they will always continue if they have the right reasons. To rationalize (tell yourself rational lies) where you are in life can cloud the real issue. This book is not about surviving today—it's about having a sound financial future. It's not about mansions and yachts. It's about having the freedom to choose. It's about do-ing things now so you can have choices later. This whole con-cept is a series of steps. Hopefully for you they are steps in the right direction. This is not just a job—this is your future you're dealing with.

To me a job is something you *have* to do. I hope that you'll give this program a real chance and, when you see the difference it can make in your life, not only right away but certainly down the road, it'll become something you want to do. The pleasure of doing this is in each small accomplishment. Each time you put something into one of these accounts, you take one more step toward controlling your future.

Make it a game. Have fun discovering which account will be your favorite. When you use the Totally Fun account, do just what the name says—use the money to just have fun. Don't think about it. Just spend it totally guilt-free. How much fun will it be building the Income Security account, knowing that when it's full you can literally take the next twelve months off and be paid for it?

A recent survey showed that two-thirds of the people asked hated their jobs and would leave if they could. Looking at both sides of this program shows that if you make it like work, odds are you'll grow to hate it and look for ways to quit. But, on the other hand, if you keep going at it with all the fun and enthusiasm you had when you started, *the incentive of being able to choose to leave your job when you want to should keep you going when times get tough*.

USE YOUR IMAGINATION

One of the key elements in creating fun in the games you play is to use your imagination. When the mind creates images during a game, it seems to enhance the game itself. You see outcomes and possibilities when you're playing that a casual observer would miss. Making a game of financial freedom can not only make it more enjoyable but in some cases actually speed up the process.

Take the Totally Fun account for instance. Let's say you emptied it out for your shopping day and there's a total of $100 in your hands. You go to some unusual stores and finally settle on something to buy. Following the guidelines that were explained earlier, you ask the store owner to hold the item for a few days and you'll return with the money to pick it up.

The first part of the fun is in the fact that you bought something simply because you wanted it. It wasn't something you needed, and spending the cash for it didn't create another financial burden. You also didn't go into debt to get it. This was truly a pure pleasure purchase. Admit it, buying for pure pleasure is fun.

Here's a way to have even more fun. I mentioned how your imagination can heighten the fun of a game. Now use your imagination to come up with a way to get another $100 to make this purchase. You can't take it from one of the other accounts. Just use your mind. Have fun creating new ways to find money. This is a good news–good news situation. The good news is, you may come up with a unique and fun way to raise some extra money. And the other good news is, if you can't, you still have fun picking up what you bought with the money from your Totally Fun account.

Another way to use your imagination is to let it come up with ways to set aside even more money. Suppose when you start this program you are able to set aside only 10 percent of your earnings to fund this program. After you get all the accounts set up, enjoy the satisfaction of what you are doing. Sit back and imagine all the things you can do once you've reached your goals. Imagine what it'll feel like to have absolutely no financial pressure of any kind on you whatsoever. Imagine being able to take an entire year off from work without worrying one bit about how you'll live, because you'll have the finances in place to live fairly well.

Now imagine being able to do it faster. Imagine filling the accounts up in half the time. Imagine creating a secure account of investments that are always profitable. Now imagine how you'd do it. Get a little crazy. Let your creativity come out. What if you came up with an idea that added another 5 percent of your income to what you're doing? That idea alone would allow you to achieve your goals 25 percent faster. Wow!

THREE IDEAS A DAY

Here's an exercise that's not only fun, but it could be extremely profitable as well. It's also easy.

Each morning when you wake up, think of three outrageous money-making ideas—the more outrageous the better. Don't even bother writing them down. The important part of this is the actual exercise. You are stretching your mind and opening up to possibilities. You are practicing creativity.

This could become important if you ever need money in an emergency. When you've been practicing being creative, it's easier to come up with ways to raise small amounts of cash quickly. Your mind becomes conditioned to quickly think of ways to create money.

The other benefit is possibilities. The reason I tell you not to write any of the ideas down is because you'll forget them by noon, and that's a good thing. But what if one idea keeps coming back? Keeps getting clearer and more defined? Expands and creates thoughts of how to accomplish it and who can help you? Let it grow.

If your ideas, as outrageous as they may be, could all create massive wealth, how many would you need to actually manifest? One really good one could make you financially free for life. Yet, if you don't do the exercise, it would be very difficult to get the one idea. And even if you get it, you may not know how to develop it. In fact, you may just let it go.

I believe you have at least one great idea—one idea that will benefit many people and reward you with wealth and security. The key is, you need to be ready when it comes or you'll miss it. Constantly allowing your mind to come up with outrageous ideas keeps you ready. When your idea appears, you're ready to accept it, help it grow, and share it with the world.

Not doing this fun exercise can cause you to miss your opportunity to benefit everyone around you. And helping others succeed is the key to long-lasting success and security for you.

FOCUSED FUN AND THE REFRIGERATOR

The most powerful key to success at anything is what I call the power of *why*. Knowing why you would do something is what keeps you going when you encounter some roadblocks or detours along the way. Anyone can show you *how* to do something, but you won't do it until you know *why* you should.

For example, this book gives you all the tools you need to eliminate your debts and secure your financial freedom. But unless you know why you're doing this, there is very little chance for success. To have anything just for the sake of having it is seldom worth the effort. However, once you know *why* you need to accomplish something, it's difficult to get discouraged enough to give up.

There are plenty of fun reasons why you'll want to succeed at attaining your financial freedom. You need to focus on them often. There will be times when you'll doubt yourself and the chances of obtaining your freedom. Often it'll be the *why* things that will get you to press on.

You may be asking yourself what "fun reasons" might be. They can be whatever you want them to be—vacations, golf clubs, wardrobes, jewelry, and the like. While these desires may be considered materialistic, you aren't focusing your life around fulfilling them. You simply imagine how much fun it would be to be able to have those things—fun because, in order to buy any of them, all of your financial obligations have to be taken care of and eliminated. It's like dessert. Once you give your body all it needs to continue operating at maximum efficiency, then you can enjoy something for the sheer pleasure of simply having it. In other words, fun!

I suggest using your refrigerator as your "fun file." Cut out some pictures of things that would be fun for you to do, see, or have, and place them on the doors. Every time you need something to eat or drink, you can focus on the fun you'll have once you've completed your goals of financial freedom. In essence, you'll truly be able to enjoy the fruits of your labor.

Our fridge is covered with pictures. Each time we achieve

one of the things we put on the refrigerator, it comes off and another one gets put in its place. We keep on dreaming of bigger and more fun things to do. This can help maintain your focus on going forward rather than becoming comfortable and risking backsliding to where you were before.

Get yourself a pair of scissors and some magazines and have some fun. Cut out pictures of anything you might want. They could be pictures of cars, boats, or planes. It could be your dream home on a lake. It could be the college of your dreams for the kids. Anything at all qualifies. One of the things that makes this really fun is the lack of rules. There are no limits to what you can dream other than the ones you put on yourself. Let yourself go and watch what happens.

The key is your imagination. When you can imagine it, it becomes a possibility. When you focus on it, it becomes a plan. When you act on it, it becomes a destination. And when you continue on it, it becomes a reality. Once it becomes a reality, you begin looking toward new horizons because that which you once thought impossible is now part of your everyday life.

When you truly believe in yourself, it becomes easy for others to believe in you.

Unknown

CHAPTER SEVENTEEN

The Two-Year Rules

When God wants to grow a squash He grows it in one summer; but when He wants to grow an oak He takes a century.

James A. Garfield

YOU CAN'T JUST TRY

By now you have hope and can see a light at the end of your financial tunnel. We've covered a lot of ground, and it would be easy to confuse some of the steps. It could also get discouraging along the road. You need to be able to focus on your destination. You need to keep going towards your financial independence. You need to just do it!

The way the multiple account system works is not an opinion. Putting all your money in one account and keeping it straight in your head or on a piece of paper simply won't work. The minute you start to focus on different ways of getting financially free, you take your focus off the very freedom you're working toward and put it on reinventing the wheel.

The whole purpose of designing the accounts the way you've seen them is to allow you to focus on the destination. My intent was to make the deposits and the rest of the process as mechanical as possible. This way you'll find it easier to stay motivated. It also goes a long way toward making saving and *paying cash* for things strong habits. Thinking about cash makes it easier to realize how it is an exchange for your labor.

When you use a credit card, debit card, or even your check-book, your thinking process is removed from what the numbers representing the dollars really mean. Remember, you are compensated for the services you render. Each minute you spend doing something needs to be rewarded. Before you spend your hard-earned cash, recall what you did to earn it. After all, you spent part of your life to get it. How much is your life worth?

There are other ways to set up your finances and, as you achieve your own financial freedom, you'll be able to design a plan that's perfect for you. I strongly suggest using this book and the guidelines in it for at least two years. At that point, you'll be closer to your destination, and you'll have developed good money habits. Your thoughts will change from "How can I get what I want now?" to "How can I get my money to produce the most for me so I can get what I want whenever I want it?"

Two years is not a long time, especially when it involves taking major steps in changing your life for the better. In relative financial terms, two years is a very short term. When you consider that most mortgages are thirty years and car loans can now be stretched to seven years, two years to break the chains of debt should be a walk in the park.

TWO-BY-TWO

Two years of financial planning is short enough to be doable and long enough to produce results. As soon as you begin this short journey, your destination can already be seen in the distance. Your success over two years is easier to see since more than one major life change in that period is unlikely.

But how do you develop a solid two-year plan? When you decide to build your financial future in two-year increments and you're just beginning, wouldn't it make sense to review the last two years as the most accurate reflection of how you really live? If you need to make adjustments in spending habits, doesn't it make sense to look back over time, rather than only use what you did last month?

Let's say that over the last year you spent an average of $2,000 a month. If you looked at last month alone, you may see that you truly needed to spend all $2,000. That could prove discouraging. But if you looked over the last two years, you may see ups and downs. For instance, one month you may have had a major home repair and spent $4,000, while the rest of the year you averaged $1,200. The likelihood of that repair happening again is small, so you can see where this extra money went.

You can spot trends over a period of two years. It is important for you to be able to see in which months your spending is higher than average. Times like back to school, holidays, and vacations may cause extra spending and raise your average. Pinpoint those areas and see if there are ways to spend less. The other thing you can do is to open an extra account and begin saving for those specific times when spending does go up. At least the interest you earn will reduce what you need to take from your income.

We all experience changes in our lives. Over the next two years you will experience more. Your children may graduate high school, go to college and leave home. These situations could cause shifts in spending. Using the most recent two years of history to plan the next could be a powerful weapon for avoiding financial emergencies.

Make copies of the two-year history found in the back of the book. Redo this history every two years, and see how much money you can redirect and put to work for your future. You will find that even when you feel you've become very efficient, as you get used to living a certain way over a two-year period, you'll discover other ways to save.

SELL, SELL, SELL

Let's have some fun. Go to the store and buy a pack of those little stick-on circles. As soon as you get home I want you to go around the house and put one sticker on anything that you haven't used in the last two years.

Can't think of anything? How about old books you've read? What about the collection of old record albums? That tool you can't seem to remember what you bought it for? All the baby stuff. Dishes you no longer use. Starting to get the picture?

Once they are all tagged, go back and put some ridiculously cheap prices on them. Gather them up and put them in the garage. Call your local paper and advertise a yard sale for next weekend. (Check your town ordinances—you may need to get a permit to do this.) Get up early and set everything out. Get ready for an interesting and fun day.

The last time I had a sale like that, I earned $150. Not a fortune, but I also found a lot more space in my house and garage, and people got super bargains on stuff they needed. Then I took the entire $150 and divided it into the six accounts. While each account didn't grow tremendously, for very little effort I became $25 closer to freedom in each part of my financial future. I reduced my debts by that amount, increased my investments by that amount, took a $25 step towards a year off, added another brick to my permanent wealth structure, and had an extra $25 to spend anyway I wanted.

Now I look forward to doing it once a year. It has become part of the spring cleaning process around the house. Anything that hasn't been used and could still benefit someone else is set aside for sale. I have fun, make some extra money, and benefit others. Truly a win-win-win situation.

Instead of a yard sale, you might consider giving away the stuff you no longer need. You could donate it to Goodwill or the Volunteers of America, for example. Give everything a value and take a tax deduction. You'll be helping those that are less fortunate, while creating more space in your house for other things you may want or need. (Check with your accountant regarding your eligibility for taking deductions on donated items.)

MOVING INVESTMENTS

One of the quickest ways I know to drive yourself crazy is to look at your long-term investments every day. For some reason we don't seem to notice the slow growth. When we see a sudden drop in value, nothing happening for a few days, or news of impending doom, we might panic and want to sell.

My purpose is not to create Wall Street wizards. There are many books on investing, and I suggest you read them for more information. If you do that, you will see many different opinions on what's happening, what's going to happen, and where the best place to put your money is. My point is, most of that information is based on someone's opinion. They never take into account *your* needs and financial goals. Read everyone's ideas, take what you need and feel comfortable with, and use it as your guide.

What if you make a mistake? That's one of the biggest benefits of having several accounts to work with and only one earmarked for investing. You can never lose it all. You will only invest what can comfortably be invested. While no one likes to lose, it's always a possibility. By having certain accounts designated for investing, the rest of your money is protected and producing for you.

Investment money should be required to work harder since you are willing to wait for a return. That means you should look for a higher interest earning than you can get elsewhere. Generally that number is about 6 to 8 percent above what regular savings will earn in a bank. Currently, banks in the United States are paying around 2 percent on money simply deposited. (I am talking about money that you can put in and take out at any time. Certificates of deposit (CDs) are different, and we'll discuss them in a moment.)

That means you should set a goal for your investment account to produce at a rate of around 10 percent. Don't get greedy. You will be attracted by investments promising 20, 30 even 50 percent on your money. Remember, the higher the potential earnings, the higher the risk. I learned where to invest by watching insurance companies. Look at the huge buildings they occupy. Do you think the money to build those came just from you paying premiums? No, they invested the premium and used the investment earnings to build monuments to their greatness.

They also understand cycles. Over long periods of time, the right place to put your money changes. In the late 1970s people who invested in long-term certificates of deposit earned high interest with security. In the early 1980s, money poured into real estate. That was followed by junk bonds, then stocks, then mutual funds, and so on. Each one of those areas eventually suffered a major downturn. Yet many fortunes were made. Why?

Timing. The investors who were successful got in and out at the right time. For the purpose of personal wealth and security, you should review your investments every two years. You should also distribute your gains into the other accounts. This way you can never lose it all. Part of your investment earnings will be yours to keep. Doing it over two years will allow for radical short-term changes to average out. For example, in one of the areas I invested, I was given a performance report every quarter. The first quarter showed I was earning at a rate of 26 percent interest. Wow! But the second quarter showed I would lose at a 3 percent rate. Had I not stuck to my plan I would have cost myself money. By the end of the two years, the average rate was 12 percent.

At the two-year mark, take what you are earning with your Totally Fun account and add 8 percent to it. That is what you should be earning with your investment account. If you didn't earn that over the two-year period, look for a long-term investment that can provide that. If you did earn it, take the profit and distribute it among the other accounts, including the percentage that should go back into your investment account. *Never "let it ride."*

One way to see where you can put your money is to play

while you wait. In the beginning stages of this process, you may not have enough to invest yet. While you are putting money into the account, pretend you have enough and invest on paper. By practicing and learning, you'll find you can do fairly well spotting long-term opportunities. You will also learn who you can go to for advice that fits your individual goals.

PART FIVE

THE MAP

A survey by the Consumer Bankers Association found that, within a year, 70 percent of the people who had shifted credit card balances to home equity were again running up credit card debt.

Unknown

CHAPTER 18

History

In order to get to your goal as quickly as possible, you need to eliminate as many mistakes as possible. Don't be too concerned about making new mistakes, because they teach you how to improve. However, don't make the same mistakes repeatedly.

Make two copies of Table 18.1, and take a look at where you spent money over the last two years. Don't include your monthly installment bills—those are just payments. (You may have spent $1,000 on clothes in June and the payments are $50 a month. If your goal is to pay cash in the future, is it more valuable to know about the $1,000 or the monthly payment?)

See where you've spent your largest sums of money. Is there any way you could have accomplished the same result and spent less? Is it possible that some of those major purchases could have been put off for a while or even eliminated altogether? Those answers are easier to come by when you have accurate figures and not minimum monthly payments to look at.

Add it all up and divide by 24 (the number of months you looked at). This is what you need to live on in order to maintain your lifestyle on a cash basis. It also makes you focus on the actual money spent rather than on the ever-tempting low monthly payment.

You may notice some surprises when you do this. You may see areas where you have spent more than you thought you did. The important thing is that you see them. Once you find them it becomes easy to do something about them. The beauty is that the changes you make don't have to be large ones.

Take food as an example. Let's say you're spending $400 a month on food. That's about $100 a week. What if you set a goal

Table 18.1 Yearly Expenditures

	Jan.	Feb.	March	April	May	June	July	Aug.	Sept.	Oct.	Nov.	Dec.
Food												
Clothes												
Auto												
Insurance												
Home												
Restaurant												
Entertainment												
Utilities												
Taxes												
Medical												
School												
Appliances												
Music												
Gas												

of feeding your family better for 5 percent less. You can succeed on two levels. Even if you don't reduce your costs, because your family is eating healthier, you may not have surprise medical costs showing up. But if you accomplish both parts of your goal, you could be saving an extra $20 a month. If you applied that just to your credit card debt, you'd pay them off even quicker.

Whatever you do, don't treat it like "found" money. That money was there all along and you worked to get it. Now that you can finally hold it without sending it away to pay bills, why not let it work for you? "But it's only $20," you say. "What could that amount to?" Let's see what happens to $20 a month when it earns 10 percent interest.

In five years you would have $1,561.65. That amount would earn you interest of $12.49 a month forever.

In ten years you would have $4,131.04, and that would pay you $33.05 a month forever.

In just fifteen years, saving $20 a month would amount to $8,358.49 and would pay you $66.87 for the rest of your life. That means if you can keep from spending $20 a month right now, it can grow to pay you back $66.87, a month and you still have the principal in the bank! That's what making your money work for you really means. And money never gets tired!

THE SIX ACCOUNTS

How much should you put into each account? The answer is entirely up to you, as long as each account gets something. While there are no wrong answers, I believe the following method is perhaps most workable.

- Add up all your monthly debt payments. (Don't include utilities and other bills—just what you owe on installments.)
- Divide the total by your family's annual income. For example, the Smiths pay $1,000 a month, or $12,000 per year, on debt. They earn $30,000.

    $12,000 ÷ $30,000 = 40%

• That is the percentage of savings that should go into your Debt Elimination account.

We'll use $30,000 as the annual income for the purposes of setting up these example accounts. That gives us $2,500 a month, which should be deposited initially in the Cash Flow account. Ten percent of that money (minimum) is to be invested in these other accounts.

The $250 could be divided like this:

Permanent Wealth Account	10% = $25
Totally Fun Account	20% = $50
Future Growth Account	10% = $25
The Year Off Account	20% = $50
Debt Elimination Account	40% = $100

These are just suggestions. Follow some of the examples that show what can happen, and then decide what you want to do.

PAYING OFF DEBTS

In the table that follows, you will see how to list your debts so that you can pay them off in the order that will help you stay encouraged and do it quicker. First you simply list all of your debts, complete with the interest rate, balance, and monthly payment. Then you put them in order, starting with the smallest balance with the highest interest rate.

DEBT	BALANCE	PAYMENT	INTEREST RATE
Visa	$3,000	$ 50	18%
Master Card	$1,000	$ 25	14%
Store	$ 500	$ 20	22%
Loan	$4,000	$179	16%

Car	$ 6,000	$315	7%
Mortgage	$75,000	$950	8%

In the Right Order

Store	$ 500	$ 20	22%
Master Card	$ 1,000	$ 25	14%
Visa	$ 3,000	$ 50	8%
Loan	$ 4,000	$179	16%
Car	$ 6,000	$315	7%
Mortgage	$75,000	$950	8%

Those monthly payments will be made from the remaining 90 percent of your income that's in the Cash Flow account. But you're also building a Debt Elimination account. By rounding numbers to keep it simple, I'll show you how powerful this account can become and why it was my favorite when I got started. In order to make it fun, I chose to pay extra on my bills only in months that ended in y. There is no science to it—that's just the way I decided to go.

If your debt picture looked like this one, here's what happens if you begin in January and look to eliminate debt quickly. First, you want to decide where to pay down. I chose to do it where I would see immediate results. That's why I started with the smallest balance and worked my way up. So in January you send in your $20 minimum payment to the store and add $100 from your Debt Elimination account. All of the $100 goes to the principal.

That would leave you with a balance of around $390 ($10 of the $20 goes to interest). In February you would repeat the process and be left with a balance of $280. There would be no extra payments in March or April, but you would pay the minimum of $20 each month. Assuming $10 of each payment went to interest, you would have a balance of $260.

In May you would make your $20 minimum payment ($10 to principal, $10 to interest). Plus you would have your $100 for

May and the contributions from March and April, for a total of
$300. That means this bill would be paid in full, with $50 left
over, by May. What do you do with the extra $50? It goes right to
the next bill on the list.

Now instead of having $100 a month going into the Debt
Elimination account, you'll have $120. Without doing the calcu-
lations here, you'll have paid the next bill off by the end of the
year. Then you'll have $145 to put into the account each month,
which should pay off the next bill the following year. That
means you would have paid off $4,500 worth of high-interest
loans in two years with the money you were already earning.

You now have $195 a month going into the Debt Elimina-
tion account. Since you were making the regular payments on
the loan and the car, they would be nearly paid off by the end of
the third year. If you add that up, you'll see that without so
much as a pay raise, you'll have $689 a month to put towards
the principal of your mortgage and still maintain your lifestyle.
In less than four more years you'll be finished with the mortgage and have over $1600 to invest in your financial freedom. I
think it's worth your trouble to fill out these two charts and see
where you can begin on your road to *total debt elimination*.

Fill out the following chart by listing every debt that you
owe. Don't worry about which one goes first until they are all
filled in. Then you can sort them out on the second chart. You
should also review this chart every now and then, especially after paying each bill—first to cross it out, and second, to see how
much closer you are to freedom.

DEBT	BALANCE	PAYMENT	INTEREST RATE

In the Right Order

Debt	Balance	Payment	Interest Rate

THIS IS WORTH IT BECAUSE . . .

When you're finished with your journey, you will be able to enjoy the fruits of your labor. But it's like when you were a child and you had to eat your vegetables before you got dessert. As much as you disliked them, knowing dessert was coming enabled you to finish all the vegetables.

Take a moment now to list all the things you'll do when freedom from debt and financial security are yours. Put them in writing and commit to getting these rewards for yourself and your family.

1. _____
2. _____
3. _____
4. _____
5. _____
6. _____
7. _____
8. _____
9. _____
10. _____

11. _____
12. _____
13. _____
14. _____
15. _____
16. _____
17. _____
18. _____
19. _____
20. _____

I commit to doing whatever it takes to accomplish the above and will continue until I've done so.

_____

Your signature and date

WHAT ABOUT THE KIDS

Most parents begin to wonder about the expense of college shortly before the children begin taking tests to see if they can get in. That leaves the family less than two years to come up with four years of tuition. You've been told before to start when they're young, but now you'll see how powerful it can be to get a few years head start.

Assume that the investment earns 10 percent and everything else is constant. Each year you are able to increase a bit until you can give $2,000 a year to the account. In the second scenario you'll see what happens when you wait to give $2,000 a year.

Investor A		Investor B	
DEPOSIT	YEAR-END BALANCE	DEPOSIT	YEAR-END BALANCE
$500	$ 550	0	0
$750	$ 1,430	0	0
$1,000	$ 2,673	0	0
$1,250	$ 4,315	0	0
$1,500	$ 6,397	0	0
$1,750	$ 8,962	0	0
0	$ 9,858	$2,000	$ 2,200
0	$10,843	$2,000	$ 4,620
0	$11,928	$2,000	$ 7,282
0	$13,121	$2,000	$10,210
0	$14,433	$2,000	$13,431

Which do you think would be easier, starting earlier while paying off your debts and putting in a little, or waiting until you can afford the $2,000 a year? Even if you were paying off your debts, you are still better off starting earlier, by about $1,000. And if you started early and didn't stop, your account would have grown to over $27,000. If you waited to start contributing $2,000, you'd have to double that to $4,000 to come within $1,000 of the starting-early scenario.

Both methods of saving for college will put you far ahead of the rest of the population. Whichever one you choose is commendable, but starting early can truly allow you to do all the things talked about in this book. Taking small steps towards several related destinations will create more satisfaction and motivation to keep going than if you complete one task over a period of time and go back to zero to start the next.

IT DOESN'T STOP HERE

If I have exposed you to the possibilities that are within your grasp, then this book is a success. I must make it clear that what you have read are not the only ways to achieve financial freedom and debt-free living. In fact, there are countless ways to make your money work for you. The more knowledge you acquire about building wealth, the more you begin to think and act like someone who is successful at getting the most from his money.

There are countless magazines and newspapers out there that provide a wealth of financial advice. Read at least one issue of each of them. Find the one that you feel is the easiest to understand, and stick with it. When you are beginning to build an investment account, that's the best time to "play" the market. You can do this with pretend money. Follow the advice of the consultants you feel good about, pretend to invest in what they say, and see how you end up.

You'll be getting a great education and probably find out that you have a better feel for investing than you may have thought. Once you are comfortable with your decisions, it's time to use real money. That'll be your report card. When you do the final tally, you'll see if you need to learn more or graduate with honors. Don't worry though. Even the experts disagree on virtually everything in finance. That means someone is wrong 50 percent of the time.

SHARING WITHOUT GIVING

As you achieve the freedom you deserve, there will be those who approach you for help. Be careful how you respond. If they have financial trouble and you can help them, be certain you offer a hand up and not a handout. Should you give them money to solve their problems, more than likely they'll return looking for more. If you keep giving to them, soon you'll join them as one of the needy.

But when you share what you've learned here and help them apply it to their own life, everyone wins. They will be able to throw the monkey of debt from their backs and prosper. You will continue growing more financially free. Both of you will be much better off—you for sharing, and they for learning and being able to share as well.

You will also be creating a lasting legacy. Your children will acquire a better way to live rather than being handed a lifestyle. They will learn through your example the importance of setting goals. They will understand the dangers of debt and the freedom one can have by avoiding it and setting up future resources before they're needed.

Their lives will have balance. The pressures of the lack of money will never burden them, while the responsibility of finance will be engrained in them. They will be able to give to the right causes and share with the right people.

The journey is challenging but worthwhile as well. I admire you for taking the first step. This is always the hardest one, and from here each step brings you closer to your dream. I salute your courage to break from the status quo and work for a better life. I hope for nothing but success and happiness for you and yours.

I know you'll make it because you're a winner. You can't fail at this unless you quit. Keep going and know that my thoughts, wishes, and prayers are for your success.

QUESTIONS YOU NEED

Ask yourself these questions every day.

1. What would I be doing now if I were already financially independent?
2. If something happened to me (injury, illness, or worse), how long would I continue to receive my income?
3. How secure is my job—really?

4. What kind of income would my family receive if I were
   to die?

5. Would I like to create a sound financial future for myself
   and my family?

I believe you now have the information you need to begin making powerful choices. Your future is beginning as this program is ending. What you do from this point forward will build your future. You choose whether it becomes the future you want. I believe in you!

CHAPTER 19

Additional Tables
and
Support Items

SOME EYE-OPENING EXAMPLES

Throughout this book I've endeavored to share the impact and hidden cost of credit. While I know that some of you were able to grasp the concept, there are others who may not be as convinced. For those of you who arc still not certain about how much instant gratification really costs you, I've included examples of actual loan calculations.

I caution you not to focus on the wrong areas. Forget about how much the loan is for. The amount of the monthly payment isn't important either. And since interest rates may be higher or lower when you're reading this, the rate doesn't make a difference in the example. What I want you to see is the time savings that occurs when you apply extra money to the principal. I want you to imagine what life would be like when you are without monthly payments.

The first example is a typical auto loan. Since most advertising is directed at new cars, I chose a 5-year or 60-month loan. I first want you to review exactly where your money goes during each of the 60 payments that you've obligated yourself to. Take a look at Table 19.1. You'll see the amount that the balance is reduced each month, and as it progresses, you'll see how much is

Table 19.1   Amortization Table

Interest	Principal	Balance	Accum. Interest	Accum. Principal	Date	Additional Payments	No.
120.00	212.13	15,787.87	120.00	212.13			1
118.41	213.72	15,574.15	238.41	425.85			2
116.81	215.32	15,358.83	355.22	641.17			3
115.19	216.94	15,141.89	470.41	858.11			4
113.56	218.57	14,923.32	583.97	1,076.68			5
111.92	220.21	14,703.11	695.89	1,296.89			6
110.27	221.86	14,481.25	806.16	1,518.75			7
108.61	223.52	14,257.73	914.77	1,742.27			8
106.93	225.20	14,032.53	1,021.70	1,967.47			9
105.24	226.89	13,805.64	1,126.94	2,194.36			10
103.54	228.59	13,577.05	1,230.48	2,422.95			11
101.83	230.30	13,346.75	1,332.31	2,653.25			12
100.10	232.03	13,114.72	1,432.41	2,885.28			13
98.36	233.77	12,880.95	1,530.77	3,119.05			14
96.61	235.52	12,645.43	1,627.38	3,354.57			15
94.84	237.29	12,408.14	1,722.22	3,591.86			16
93.06	239.07	12,169.07	1,815.28	3,830.93			17
91.27	240.86	11,928.21	1,906.55	4,071.79			18
89.46	242.67	11,685.54	1,996.01	4,314.46			19
87.64	244.49	11,441.05	2,083.65	4,558.95			20
85.81	246.32	11,194.73	2,169.46	4,805.27			21
83.96	248.17	10,946.56	2,253.42	5,053.44			22
82.10	250.03	10,696.53	2,335.52	5,303.47			23
80.22	251.91	10,444.62	2,415.74	5,555.38			24
78.33	253.80	10,190.82	2,494.07	5,809.18			25
76.43	255.70	9,935.12	2,570.50	6,064.88			26
74.51	257.62	9,677.50	2,645.01	6,322.50			27
72.58	259.55	9,417.95	2,717.59	6,582.05			28
70.63	261.50	9,156.45	2,788.22	6,843.55			29
68.67	263.46	8,892.99	2,856.89	7,107.01			30

Table 19.1   (Continued)

Interest	Principal	Balance	Accum. Interest	Accum. Principal	Date	Additional Payments	No.
66.70	265.43	8,627.56	2,923.59	7,372.44			31
64.71	267.42	8,360.14	2,988.30	7,639.86			32
62.70	269.43	8,090.71	3,051.00	7,909.29			33
60.68	271.45	7,819.26	3,111.68	8,180.74			34
58.64	273.49	7,545.77	3,170.32	8,454.23			35
56.59	275.54	7,270.23	3,226.91	8,729.77			36
54.53	277.60	6,992.63	3,281.44	9,007.37			37
52.44	279.69	6,712.94	3,333.88	9,287.06			38
50.35	281.78	6,431.16	3,384.23	9,568.84			39
48.23	283.90	6,147.26	3,432.46	9,852.74			40
46.10	286.03	5,861.23	3,478.56	10,138.77			41
43.96	288.17	5,573.06	3,522.52	10,426.94			42
41.80	290.33	5,282.73	3,564.32	10,717.27			43
39.62	292.51	4,990.22	3,603.94	11,009.78			44
37.43	294.70	4,695.52	3,641.37	11,304.48			45
35.22	296.91	4,398.61	3,676.59	11,601.39			46
32.99	299.14	4,099.47	3,709.58	11,900.53			47
30.75	301.38	3,798.09	3,740.33	12,201.91			48
28.49	303.64	3,494.45	3,768.82	12,505.55			49
26.21	305.92	3,188.53	3,795.03	12,811.47			50
23.91	308.22	2,880.31	3,818.94	13,119.69			51
21.60	310.53	2,569.78	3,840.54	13,430.22			52
19.27	312.86	2,256.92	3,859.81	13,743.08			53
16.93	315.20	1,941.72	3,876.74	14,058.28			54
14.56	317.57	1,624.15	3,891.30	14,375.85			55
12.18	319.95	1,304.20	3,903.48	14,695.80			56
9.78	322.35	981.85	3,913.26	15,018.15			57
7.36	324.77	657.08	3,920.62	15,342.92			58
4.93	327.20	329.88	3,925.55	15,670.12			50
2.47	329.88	0.00	3,928.02	16,000.00			60

applied to the amount you've borrowed. In this case, the original loan amount is $16,000.

Then I imagined that the only extra payments you could make would be from your Debt Elimination account, and they would be made every three months. In Table 19.2 you will see an additional payment made every three months. Since that is an extra payment, the entire amount is applied to principal. Look at the difference in the time it takes to pay the loan off.

THE ULTIMATE GOAL

While some of you may not be in the market for a home just yet, others may have a mortgage as their final large debt. The following example will show just how powerful it can be to finally take control of your finances. I hope it serves as a goal for you to eliminate all of your other obligations so that you can apply at least double your mortgage payments to the loan.

I've included Table 19.3, which shows every single payment, because I want you to keep focused on what kind of commitment you've made. You really need to focus on what it will be like to make 360 payments. You should picture what you'll be doing 30 years from now as the last payment is being made. Read every page of Table 19.3 see each payment, and I hope you'll feel uncomfortable.

Now consider this: After one full year, you've sent the bank or mortgage company $8,805.12. However, if you look at the table, under Accumulated Principal, you'll see that only $833.30, or less than 10 percent of your payments, went toward the balance. That means that over 90 percent of your money went to pay interest.

The average American moves every seven years. In that time you would have sent them $61,635.84. And yet of the $100,000 you borrowed, you'd still owe $92,477.95. That means that after seven years of paying on time every month, nearly 88 percent of your money went toward interest. What

Table 19.2   Amortization Table

Interest	Principal	Balance	Accum. Interest	Accum. Principal	Date	Additional Payments	No.
120.00	212.13	15,787.87	120.00	212.13			1
118.41	213.72	15,574.15	238.41	425.85			2
116.81	547.45	15,026.70	355.22	973.30		332.13	3
112.70	219.43	14,807.27	467.92	1,192.73			4
111.05	221.08	14,586.19	578.97	1,413.81			5
109.40	554.86	14,031.33	688.37	1,968.67		332.13	6
105.23	226.90	13,804.43	793.60	2,195.57			7
103.53	228.60	13,575.83	897.13	2,424.17			8
101.82	562.44	13,013.39	998.95	2,986.61		332.13	9
97.60	234.53	12,778.86	1,096.55	3,221.14			10
95.84	236.29	12,542.57	1,192.39	3,457.43			11
94.07	570.19	11,972.38	1,286.46	4,027.62		332.13	12
89.79	242.34	11,730.04	1,376.25	4,269.96			13
87.98	244.15	11,485.89	1,464.23	4,514.11			14
86.14	578.12	10,907.77	1,550.37	5,092.23		332.13	15
81.81	250.32	10,657.45	1,632.18	5,342.55			16
79.93	252.20	10,405.25	1,712.11	5,594.75			17
78.04	586.22	9,819.03	1,790.15	6,180.97		332.13	18
73.64	258.49	9,560.54	1,863.79	6,439.46			19
71.70	260.43	9,300.11	1,935.49	6,699.89			20
69.75	594.51	8,705.60	2,005.24	7,294.40		332.13	21
65.29	266.84	8,438.76	2,070.53	7,561.24			22
63.29	268.84	8,169.92	2,133.82	7,830.08			23
61.27	602.99	7,566.93	2,195.09	8,433.07		332.13	24
56.75	275.38	7,291.55	2,251.84	8,708.45			25
54.69	277.44	7,014.11	2,306.53	8,985.89			26
52.61	611.65	6,402.46	2,359.14	9,597.54		332.13	27
48.02	284.11	6,118.35	2,407.16	9,881.65			28
45.89	286.24	5,832.11	2,453.05	10,167.89			29
43.74	620.52	5,211.59	2,496.79	10,788.41		332.13	30

(Continued)

Table 19.2   (Continued)

Interest	Principal	Balance	Accum. Interest	Accum. Principal	Date	Additional Payments	No.
39.09	293.04	4,918.55	2,535.88	11,081.45			31
36.89	295.24	4,623.31	2,572.77	11,376.69			32
34.67	629.59	3,993.72	2,607.44	12,006.28		332.13	33
29.95	302.18	3,691.54	2,637.39	12,308.46			34
27.69	304.44	3,387.10	2,665.08	12,612.90			35
25.40	638.86	2,748.24	2,690.48	13,251.76		332.13	36
20.61	311.52	2,436.72	2,711.09	13,563.28			37
18.28	313.85	2,122.87	2,729.37	13,877.13			38
15.92	648.34	1,474.53	2,745.29	14,525.47		332.13	39
11.06	321.07	1,153.46	2,756.35	14,846.54			40
8.65	323.48	829.98	2,765.00	15,170.02			41
6.22	658.04	171.94	2,771.22	15,828.06		332.13	42
1.29	171.94	0.00	2,772.51	16,000.00			43
							44
							45
							46
							47
							48
							49
							50
							51
							52
							53
							54
							55
							56
							57
							59
							59
							60

Table 19.3   Amortization Table

Interest	Principal	Balance	Accum. Interest	Accum. Principal	Date	Additional Payments	No.
666.67	67.09	99,932.91	666.67	67.09			1
666.22	67.54	99,865.37	1,332.89	134.63			2
665.77	67.99	99,797.38	1,998.66	202.62			3
665.32	68.44	99,728.94	2,663.98	271.06			4
664.86	68.90	99,660.04	3,328.84	339.96			5
664.40	69.36	99,590.68	3,993.24	409.32			6
663.94	69.82	99,520.86	4,657.18	479.14			7
663.47	70.29	99,450.57	5,320.65	549.43			8
663.00	70.76	99,379.81	5,983.65	620.19			9
662.53	71.23	99,308.58	6,646.18	691.42			10
662.06	71.70	99,236.88	7,308.24	763.12			11
661.58	72.18	99,164.70	7,969.82	835.30			12
661.10	72.66	99,092.04	8,630.92	907.96			13
660.61	73.15	99,018.89	9,291.53	981.11			14
660.13	73.63	98,945.26	9,951.66	1,054.74			15
659.64	74.12	98,871.14	10,611.30	1,128.86			16
659.14	74.62	98,796.52	11,270.44	1,203.48			17
658.64	75.12	98,721.40	11,929.08	1,278.60			18
658.14	75.62	98,645.78	12,587.22	1,354.22			19
657.64	76.12	98,569.66	13,244.86	1,430.34			20
657.13	76.63	98,493.03	13,901.99	1,506.97			21
656.62	77.14	98,415.89	14,558.61	1,584.11			22
656.11	77.65	98,338.24	15,214.72	1,661.76			23
655.59	78.17	98,260.07	15,870.31	1,739.93			24
655.07	78.69	98,181.38	16,525.38	1,818.62			25
654.54	79.22	98,102.16	17,179.92	1,897.84			26
654.01	79.75	98,022.41	17,833.93	1,977.59			27
653.48	80.28	97,942.13	18,487.41	2,057.87			28
652.95	80.81	97,861.32	19,140.36	2,138.68			29
652.41	81.35	97,779.97	19,792.77	2,220.03			30

(Continued)

Table 19.3 (Continued)

Interest	Principal	Balance	Accum. Interest	Accum. Principal	Date	Additional Payments	No.
651.87	81.89	97,698.08	20,444.64	2,301.92			31
651.32	82.44	97,615.64	21,095.96	2,384.36			32
650.77	82.99	97,532.65	21,746.73	2,467.35			33
650.22	83.54	97,449.11	22,396.95	2,550.89			34
649.66	84.10	97,365.01	23,046.61	2,634.99			35
649.10	84.66	97,280.35	23,695.71	2,719.65			36
648.54	85.22	97,195.13	24,344.25	2,804.87			37
647.97	85.79	97,109.34	24,992.22	2,890.66			38
647.40	86.36	97,022.98	25,639.62	2,977.02			39
646.82	86.94	96,936.04	26,286.44	3,063.96			40
646.24	87.52	96,848.52	26,932.68	3,151.48			41
645.66	88.10	96,760.42	27,578.34	3,239.58			42
645.07	88.69	96,671.73	28,223.41	3,328.27			43
644.48	89.28	96,582.45	28,867.89	3,417.55			44
643.88	89.88	96,492.57	29,511.77	3,507.43			45
643.28	90.48	96,402.09	30,155.05	3,597.91			46
642.68	91.08	96,311.01	30,797.73	3,688.99			47
642.07	91.69	96,219.32	31,439.80	3,780.68			48
641.46	92.30	96,127.02	32,081.26	3,872.98			49
640.85	92.91	96,034.11	32,722.11	3,965.89			50
640.23	93.53	95,940.58	33,362.34	4,059.42			51
639.60	94.16	95,846.42	34,001.94	4,153.58			52
638.98	94.78	95,751.64	34,640.92	4,248.36			53
638.34	95.42	95,656.22	35,279.26	4,343.78			54
637.71	96.05	95,560.17	35,916.97	4,439.83			55
637.07	96.69	95,463.48	36,554.04	4,536.52			56
636.42	97.34	95,366.14	37,190.46	4,633.86			57
635.77	97.99	95,268.15	37,826.23	4,731.85			58
635.12	98.64	95,169.51	38,461.35	4,830.49			59
634.46	99.30	95,070.21	39,095.81	4,929.79			60

Table 19.3   (Continued)

Interest	Principal	Balance	Accum. Interest	Accum. Principal	Date	Additional Payments	No.
633.80	99.96	94,970.25	39,729.61	5,029.75			61
633.14	100.62	94,869.63	40,362.75	5,130.37			62
632.46	101.30	94,768.33	40,995.21	5,231.67			63
631.79	101.97	94,666.36	41,627.00	5,333.64			64
631.11	102.65	94,563.71	42,258.11	5,436.29			65
630.42	103.34	94,460.37	42,888.53	5,539.63			66
629.74	104.02	94,356.35	43,518.27	5,643.65			67
629.04	104.72	94,251.63	44,147.31	5,748.37			68
628.34	105.42	94,146.21	44,775.65	5,853.79			69
627.64	106.12	94,040.09	45,403.29	5,959.91			70
626.93	106.83	93,933.26	46,030.22	6,066.74			71
626.22	107.54	93,825.72	46,656.44	6,174.28			72
625.50	108.26	93,717.46	47,281.94	6,282.54			73
624.78	108.98	93,608.48	47,906.72	6,391.52			74
624.06	109.70	93,498.78	48,530.78	6,501.22			75
623.33	110.43	93,388.35	49,154.11	6,611.65			76
622.59	111.17	93,277.18	49,776.70	6,722.82			77
621.85	111.91	93,165.27	50,398.55	6,834.73			78
621.10	112.66	93,052.61	51,019.65	6,947.39			79
620.35	113.41	92,939.20	51,640.00	7,060.80			80
619.59	114.17	92,825.03	52,259.59	7,174.97			81
618.83	114.93	92,710.10	52,878.42	7,289.90			82
618.07	115.69	92,594.41	53,496.49	7,405.59			83
617.30	116.46	92,477.95	54,113.79	7,522.05			84
616.52	117.24	92,360.71	54,730.31	7,639.29			85
615.74	118.02	92,242.69	55,346.05	7,757.31			86
614.95	118.81	92,123.88	55,961.00	7,876.12			87
614.16	119.60	92,004.28	56,575.16	7,995.72			88
613.36	120.40	91,883.88	57,188.52	8,116.12			89
612.56	121.20	91,762.68	57,801.08	8,237.32			90

(Continued)

Table 19.3 (Continued)

Interest	Principal	Balance	Accum. Interest	Accum. Principal	Date	Additional Payments	No.
611.75	122.01	91,640.67	58,412.83	8,359.33			91
610.94	122.82	91,517.85	59,023.77	8,482.15			92
610.12	123.64	91,394.21	59,633.89	8,605.79			93
609.29	124.47	91,269.74	60,243.18	8,730.26			94
608.46	125.30	91,144.44	60,851.64	8,855.56			95
607.63	126.13	91,018.31	61,459.27	8,981.69			96
606.79	126.97	90,891.34	62,066.06	9,108.66			97
605.94	127.82	90,763.52	62,672.00	9,236.48			98
605.09	128.67	90,634.85	63,277.09	9,365.15			99
604.23	129.53	90,505.32	63,881.32	9,494.68			100
603.37	130.39	90,374.93	64,484.69	9,625.07			101
602.50	131.26	90,243.67	65,087.19	9,756.33			102
601.62	132.14	90,111.53	65,688.81	9,888.47			103
600.74	133.02	89,978.51	66,289.55	10,021.49			104
599.86	133.90	89,844.61	66,889.41	10,155.39			105
598.96	134.80	89,709.81	67,488.37	10,290.19			106
598.07	135.69	89,574.12	68,086.44	10,425.88			107
597.16	136.60	89,437.52	68,683.60	10,562.48			108
596.25	137.51	89,300.01	69,279.85	10,699.99			109
595.33	138.43	89,161.58	69,875.18	10,838.42			110
594.41	139.35	89,022.23	70,469.59	10,977.77			111
593.48	140.28	88,881.95	71,063.07	11,118.05			112
592.55	141.21	88,740.74	71,655.62	11,259.26			113
591.60	142.16	88,598.58	72,247.22	11,401.42			114
590.66	143.10	88,455.48	72,837.88	11,544.52			115
589.70	144.06	88,311.42	73,427.58	11,688.58			116
588.74	145.02	88,166.40	74,016.32	11,833.60			117
587.78	145.98	88,020.42	74,604.10	11,979.58			118
586.80	146.96	87,873.46	75,190.90	12,126.54			119
585.82	147.94	87,725.52	75,776.72	12,274.48			120

Table 19.3   (Continued)

Interest	Principal	Balance	Accum. Interest	Accum. Principal	Date	Additional Payments	No.
584.84	148.92	87,576.60	76,361.56	12,423.40			121
583.84	149.92	87,426.68	76,945.40	12,573.32			122
582.84	150.92	87,275.76	77,528.24	12,724.24			123
581.84	151.92	87,123.84	78,110.08	12,876.16			124
580.83	152.93	86,970.91	78,690.91	13,029.09			125
579.81	153.95	86,816.96	79,270.72	13,183.04			126
578.78	154.98	86,661.98	79,849.50	13,338.02			127
577.75	156.01	86,505.97	80,427.25	13,494.03			128
576.71	157.05	86,348.92	81,003.96	13,651.08			129
575.66	158.10	86,190.82	81,579.62	13,809.18			130
574.61	159.15	86,031.67	82,154.23	13,968.33			131
573.54	160.22	85,871.45	82,727.77	14,128.55			132
572.48	161.28	85,710.17	83,300.25	14,289.83			133
571.40	162.36	85,547.81	83,871.65	14,452.19			134
570.32	163.44	85,384.37	84,441.97	14,615.63			135
569.23	164.53	85,219.84	85,011.20	14,780.16			136
568.13	165.63	85,054.21	85,579.33	14,945.79			137
567.03	166.73	84,887.48	86,146.36	15,112.52			138
565.92	167.84	84,719.64	86,712.28	15,280.36			139
564.80	168.96	84,550.68	87,277.08	15,449.32			140
563.67	170.09	84,380.59	87,840.75	15,619.41			141
562.54	171.22	84,209.37	88,403.29	15,790.63			142
561.40	172.36	84,037.01	88,964.69	15,962.99			143
560.25	173.51	83,863.50	89,524.94	16,136.50			144
559.09	174.67	83,688.83	90,084.03	16,311.17			145
557.93	175.83	83,513.00	90,641.96	16,487.00			146
556.75	177.01	83,335.99	91,198.71	16,664.01			147
555.57	178.19	83,157.80	91,754.28	16,842.20			148
554.39	179.37	82,978.43	92,308.67	17,021.57			149
553.19	180.57	82,797.86	92,861.86	17,202.14			150

(Continued)

Table 19.3 (Continued)

Interest	Principal	Balance	Accum. Interest	Accum. Principal	Date	Additional Payments	No.
551.99	181.77	82,616.09	93,413.85	17,383.91			151
550.77	182.99	82,433.10	93,964.62	17,566.90			152
549.55	184.21	82,248.89	94,514.17	17,751.11			153
548.33	185.43	82,063.46	95,062.50	17,936.54			154
547.09	186.67	81,876.79	95,609.59	18,123.21			155
545.85	187.91	81,688.88	96,155.44	18,311.12			156
544.59	189.17	81,499.71	96,700.03	18,500.29			157
543.33	190.43	81,309.28	97,243.36	18,690.72			158
542.06	191.70	81,117.58	97,785.42	18,882.42			159
540.78	192.98	80,924.60	98,326.20	19,075.40			160
539.50	194.26	80,730.34	98,865.70	19,269.66			161
538.20	195.56	80,534.78	99,403.90	19,465.22			162
536.90	196.86	80,337.92	99,940.80	19,662.08			163
535.59	198.17	80,139.75	100,476.39	19,860.25			164
534.27	199.49	79,940.26	101,010.66	20,059.74			165
532.94	200.82	79,739.44	101,543.60	20,260.56			166
531.60	202.16	79,537.28	102,075.20	20,462.72			167
530.25	203.51	79,333.77	102,605.45	20,666.23			168
528.89	204.87	79,128.90	103,134.34	20,871.10			169
527.53	206.23	78,922.67	103,661.87	21,077.33			170
526.15	207.61	78,715.06	104,188.02	21,284.94			171
524.77	208.99	78,506.07	104,712.79	21,493.93			172
523.37	210.39	78,295.68	105,236.16	21,704.32			173
521.97	211.79	78,083.89	105,758.13	21,916.11			174
520.56	213.20	77,870.69	106,278.69	22,129.31			175
519.14	214.62	77,656.07	106,797.83	22,343.93			176
517.71	216.05	77,440.02	107,315.54	22,559.98			177
516.27	217.49	77,222.53	107,831.81	22,777.47			178
514.82	218.94	77,003.59	108,346.63	22,996.41			179
513.36	220.40	76,783.19	108,859.99	23,216.81			180

Table 19.3   (Continued)

Interest	Principal	Balance	Accum. Interest	Accum. Principal	Date	Additional Payments	No.
511.89	221.87	76,561.32	109,371.88	23,438.68			181
510.41	223.35	76,337.97	109,882.29	23,662.03			182
508.92	224.84	76,113.13	110,391.21	23,886.87			183
507.42	226.34	75,886.79	110,898.63	24,113.21			184
505.91	227.85	75,658.94	111,404.54	24,341.06			185
504.39	229.37	75,429.57	111,908.93	24,570.43			186
502.86	230.90	75,198.67	112,411.79	24,801.33			187
501.32	232.44	74,966.23	112,913.11	25,033.77			188
499.77	233.99	74,732.24	113,412.88	25,267.76			189
498.21	235.55	74,496.69	113,911.09	25,503.31			190
496.64	237.12	74,259.57	114,407.73	25,740.43			191
495.06	238.70	74,020.87	114,902.79	25,979.13			192
493.47	240.29	73,780.58	115,396.26	26,219.42			193
491.87	241.89	73,538.69	115,888.13	26,461.31			194
490.26	243.50	73,295.19	116,378.39	26,704.81			195
488.63	245.13	73,050.06	116,867.02	26,949.94			196
487.00	246.76	72,803.30	117,354.02	27,196.70			197
485.36	248.40	72,554.90	117,839.38	27,445.10			198
483.70	250.06	72,304.84	118,323.08	27,695.16			199
482.03	251.73	72,053.11	118,805.11	27,946.89			200
480.35	253.41	71,799.70	119,285.46	28,200.30			201
478.66	255.10	71,544.60	119,764.12	28,455.40			202
476.96	256.80	71,287.80	120,241.08	28,712.20			203
475.25	258.51	71,029.29	120,716.33	28,970.71			204
473.53	260.23	70,769.06	121,189.86	29,230.94			205
471.79	261.97	70,507.09	121,661.65	29,492.91			206
470.05	263.71	70,243.38	122,131.70	29,756.62			207
468.29	265.47	69,977.91	122,599.99	30,022.09			208
466.52	267.24	69,710.67	123,066.51	30,289.33			209
464.74	269.02	69,441.65	123,531.25	30,558.35			210

(Continued)

Table 19.3 (Continued)

Interest	Principal	Balance	Accum. Interest	Accum. Principal	Date	Additional Payments	No.
462.94	270.82	69,170.83	123,994.19	30,829.17			211
461.14	272.62	68,898.21	124,455.33	31,101.79			212
459.32	274.44	68,623.77	124,914.65	31,376.23			213
457.49	276.27	68,347.50	125,372.14	31,652.50			214
455.65	278.11	68,069.39	125,827.79	31,930.61			215
453.80	279.96	67,789.43	126,281.59	32,210.57			216
451.93	281.83	67,507.60	126,733.52	32,492.40			217
450.05	283.71	67,223.89	127,183.57	32,776.11			218
448.16	285.60	66,938.29	127,631.73	33,061.71			219
446.26	287.50	66,650.79	128,077.99	33,349.21			220
444.34	289.42	66,361.37	128,522.33	33,638.63			221
442.41	291.35	66,070.02	128,964.74	33,929.98			222
440.47	293.29	65,776.73	129,405.21	34,223.27			223
438.51	295.25	65,481.48	129,843.72	34,518.52			224
436.54	297.22	65,184.26	130,280.26	34,815.74			225
434.56	299.20	64,885.06	130,714.82	35,114.94			226
432.57	301.19	64,583.87	131,147.39	35,416.13			227
430.56	303.20	64,280.67	131,577.95	35,719.33			228
428.54	305.22	63,975.45	132,006.49	36,024.55			229
426.50	307.26	63,668.19	132,432.99	36,331.81			230
424.45	309.31	63,358.88	132,857.44	36,641.12			231
422.39	311.37	63,047.51	133,279.83	36,952.49			232
420.32	313.44	62,734.07	133,700.15	37,265.93			233
418.23	315.53	62,418.54	134,118.38	37,581.46			234
416.12	317.64	62,100.90	134,534.50	37,899.10			235
414.01	319.75	61,781.15	134,948.51	38,218.85			236
411.87	321.89	61,459.26	135,360.38	38,540.74			237
409.73	324.03	61,135.23	135,770.11	38,864.77			238
407.57	326.19	60,809.04	136,177.68	39,190.96			239
405.39	328.37	60,480.67	136,583.07	39,519.33			240

Table 19.3   (Continued)

Interest	Principal	Balance	Accum. Interest	Accum. Principal	Date	Additional Payments	No.
403.20	330.56	60,150.11	136,986.27	39,849.89			241
401.00	332.76	59,817.35	137,387.27	40,182.65			242
398.78	334.98	59,482.37	137,786.05	40,517.63			243
396.55	337.21	59,145.16	138,182.60	40,854.84			244
394.30	339.46	58,805.70	138,576.90	41,194.30			245
392.04	341.72	58,463.98	138,968.94	41,536.02			246
389.76	344.00	58,119.98	139,358.70	41,880.02			247
387.47	346.29	57,773.69	139,746.17	42,226.31			248
385.16	348.60	57,425.09	140,131.33	42,574.91			249
382.83	350.93	57,074.16	140,514.16	42,925.84			250
380.49	353.27	56,720.89	140,894.65	43,279.11			251
378.14	355.62	56,365.27	141,272.79	43,634.73			252
375.77	357.99	56,007.28	141,648.56	43,992.72			253
373.38	360.38	55,646.90	142,021.94	44,353.10			254
370.98	362.78	55,284.12	142,392.92	44,715.88			255
368.56	365.20	54,918.92	142,761.48	45,081.08			256
366.13	367.63	54,551.29	143,127.61	45,448.71			257
363.68	370.08	54,181.21	143,491.29	45,818.79			258
361.21	372.55	53,808.66	143,852.50	46,191.34			259
358.72	375.04	53,433.62	144,211.22	46,566.38			260
356.22	377.54	53,056.08	144,567.44	46,943.92			261
353.71	380.05	52,676.03	144,921.15	47,323.97			262
351.17	382.59	52,293.44	145,272.32	47,706.56			263
348.62	385.14	51,908.30	145,620.94	48,091.70			264
346.06	387.70	51,520.60	145,967.00	48,479.40			265
343.47	390.29	51,130.31	146,310.47	48,869.69			266
340.87	392.89	50,737.42	146,651.34	49,262.58			267
338.25	395.51	50,341.91	146,989.59	49,658.09			268
335.61	398.15	49,943.76	147,325.20	50,056.24			269
332.96	400.80	49,542.96	147,658.16	50,457.04			270

(Continued)

Table 19.3   (Continued)

Interest	Principal	Balance	Accum. Interest	Accum. Principal	Date	Additional Payments	No.
330.29	403.47	49,139.49	147,988.45	50,860.51			271
327.60	406.16	48,733.33	148,316.05	51,266.67			272
324.89	408.87	48,324.46	148,640.94	51,675.54			273
322.16	411.60	47,912.86	148,963.10	52,087.14			274
319.42	414.34	47,498.52	149,282.52	52,501.48			275
316.66	417.10	47,081.42	149,599.18	52,918.58			276
313.88	419.88	46,661.54	149,913.06	53,338.46			277
311.08	422.68	46,238.86	150,224.14	53,761.14			278
308.26	425.50	45,813.36	150,532.40	54,186.64			279
305.42	428.34	45,385.02	150,837.82	54,614.98			280
302.57	431.19	44,953.83	151,140.39	55,046.17			281
299.69	434.07	44,519.76	151,440.08	55,480.24			282
296.80	436.96	44,082.80	151,736.88	55,917.20			283
293.89	439.87	43,642.93	152,030.77	56,357.07			284
290.95	442.81	43,200.12	152,321.72	56,799.88			285
288.00	445.76	42,754.36	152,609.72	57,245.64			286
285.03	448.73	42,305.63	152,894.75	57,694.37			287
282.04	451.72	41,853.91	153,176.79	58,146.09			288
279.03	454.73	41,399.18	153,455.82	58,600.82			289
275.99	457.77	40,941.41	153,731.81	59,058.59			290
272.94	460.82	40,480.59	154,004.75	59,519.41			291
269.87	463.89	40,016.70	154,274.62	59,983.30			292
266.78	466.98	39,549.72	154,541.40	60,450.28			293
263.66	470.10	39,079.62	154,805.06	60,920.38			294
260.53	473.23	38,606.39	155,065.59	61,393.61			295
257.38	476.38	38,130.01	155,322.97	61,869.99			296
254.20	479.56	37,650.45	155,577.17	62,349.55			297
251.00	482.76	37,167.69	155,828.17	62,832.31			298
247.78	485.98	36,681.71	156,075.95	63,318.29			299
244.54	489.22	36,192.49	156,320.49	63,807.51			300

Table 19.3 (Continued)

Interest	Principal	Balance	Accum. Interest	Accum. Principal	Date	Additional Payments	No.
241.28	492.48	35,700.01	156,561.77	64,299.99			301
238.00	495.76	35,204.25	156,799.77	64,795.75			302
234.70	499.06	34,705.19	157,034.47	65,294.81			303
231.37	502.39	34,202.80	157,265.84	65,797.20			304
228.02	505.74	33,697.06	157,493.86	66,302.94			305
224.65	509.11	33,187.95	157,718.51	66,812.05			306
221.25	512.51	32,675.44	157,939.76	67,324.56			307
217.84	515.92	32,159.52	158,157.60	67,840.48			308
214.40	519.36	31,640.16	158,372.00	68,359.84			309
210.93	522.83	31,117.33	158,582.93	68,882.67			310
207.45	526.31	30,591.02	158,790.38	69,408.98			311
203.94	529.82	30,061.20	158,994.32	69,938.80			312
200.41	533.35	29,527.85	159,194.73	70,472.15			313
196.85	536.91	28,990.94	159,391.58	71,009.06			314
193.27	540.49	28,450.45	159,584.85	71,549.55			315
189.67	544.09	27,906.36	159,774.52	72,093.64			316
186.04	547.72	27,358.64	159,960.56	72,641.36			317
182.39	551.37	26,807.27	160,142.95	73,192.73			318
178.72	555.04	26,252.23	160,321.67	73,747.77			319
175.01	558.75	25,693.48	160,496.68	74,306.52			320
171.29	562.47	25,131.01	160,667.97	74,868.99			321
167.54	566.22	24,564.79	160,835.51	75,435.21			322
163.77	569.99	23,994.80	160,999.28	76,005.20			323
159.97	573.79	23,421.01	161,159.25	76,578.99			324
156.14	577.62	22,843.39	161,315.39	77,156.61			325
152.29	581.47	22,261.92	161,467.68	77,738.08			326
148.41	585.35	21,676.57	161,616.09	78,323.43			327
144.51	589.25	21,087.32	161,760.60	78,912.68			328
140.58	593.18	20,494.14	161,901.18	79,505.86			329
136.63	597.13	19,897.01	162,037.81	80,102.99			330

(Continued)

Table 19.3   (Continued)

Interest	Principal	Balance	Accum. Interest	Accum. Principal	Date	Additional Payments	No.
132.65	601.11	19,295.90	162,170.46	80,704.10			331
128.64	605.12	18,690.78	162,299.10	81,309.22			332
124.61	609.15	18,081.63	162,423.71	81,918.37			333
120.54	613.22	17,468.41	162,544.25	82,531.59			334
116.46	617.30	16,851.11	162,660.71	83,148.89			335
112.34	621.42	16,229.69	162,773.05	83,770.31			336
108.20	625.56	15,604.13	162,881.25	84,395.87			337
104.03	629.73	14,974.40	162,985.28	85,025.60			338
99.83	633.93	14,340.47	163,085.11	85,659.53			339
95.60	638.16	13,702.31	163,180.71	86,297.69			340
91.35	642.41	13,059.90	163,272.06	86,940.10			341
87.07	646.69	12,413.21	163,359.13	87,586.79			342
82.75	651.01	11,762.20	163,441.88	88,237.80			343
78.41	655.35	11,106.85	163,520.29	88,893.15			344
74.05	659.71	10,447.14	163,594.34	89,552.86			345
69.65	664.11	9,783.03	163,663.99	90,216.97			346
65.22	668.54	9,114.49	163,729.21	90,885.51			347
60.76	673.00	8,441.49	163,789.97	91,558.51			348
56.28	677.48	7,764.01	163,846.25	92,235.99			349
51.76	682.00	7,082.01	163,898.01	92,917.99			350
47.21	686.55	6,395.46	163,945.22	93,604.54			351
42.64	691.12	5,704.34	163,987.86	94,295.66			352
38.03	695.73	5,008.61	164,025.89	94,991.39			353
33.39	700.37	4,308.24	164,059.28	95,691.76			354
28.72	705.04	3,603.20	164,088.00	96,396.80			355
24.02	709.74	2,893.46	164,112.02	97,106.54			356
19.29	714.47	2,178.99	164,131.31	97,821.01			357
14.53	719.23	1,459.76	164,145.84	98,540.24			358
9.73	724.03	735.73	164,155.57	99,264.27			359
4.90	735.73	0.00	164,160.52	100,000.00			360

this should tell you is that low-interest loans are a great deal only if you stay there for the length of the loan.

The other point you need to see is the total of payments that you'll make if you take this loan to term. To pay off this $100,000 loan, is you'll have to spend $264,160.47 over 30 years. What's important to note, however, is that you'll have to earn about $366,000 just to pay for it. Look at each and every page of the table and see if this seems like a good deal.

Find your balance after being there for five years. Ten years. Fifteen years. It's hard to believe that more people aren't made aware of the consequences of financing for such a long period of time. However, the charts that follow these will offer an alternative.

FREEDOM IN LESS THAN A THIRD OF THE TIME

There is nothing wrong with taking out a 30-year mortgage on your home. For many of you that is the only way you can qualify, in the bank's opinion. However, you can review the contracts and fine print all you want, but you won't find anything that says you must make all the payments over 30 years. In fact, you can make as many payments as you like, as long as you make at least one every month.

If you follow the suggestions outlined in this book, you'll be able to at least double your mortgage payments. The results shown in Table 19.4 will speak for themselves. What may not be as clear are the options you create for yourself and your family by striving to achieve this part of the program.

While I'm not here to predict the price of homes, I can look back at history and say that it is certainly possible to repeat itself. From the mid 1980s to the early 1990s, real estate prices in this country actually went down in many cases. This was due to a poor economy that was in a deep recession. What would happen to your home if you were paying for it by following the normal rules?

Look at the chart and see where you'd be after two years

Table 19.4   Amortization Table

Interest	Principal	Balance	Accum. Interest	Accum. Principal	Date	Additional Payments	No.
666.67	800.85	99,199.15	666.67	800.85		733.76	1
661.33	806.19	98,392.96	1,328.00	1,607.04		733.76	2
655.95	811.57	97,581.39	1,983.95	2,418.61		733.76	3
650.54	816.98	96,764.41	2,634.49	3,235.59		733.76	4
645.10	822.42	95,941.99	3,279.59	4,058.01		733.76	5
639.61	827.91	95,114.08	3,919.20	4,885.92		733.76	6
634.09	833.43	94,280.65	4,553.29	5,719.35		733.76	7
628.54	838.98	93,441.67	5,181.83	6,558.33		733.76	8
622.94	844.58	92,597.09	5,804.77	7,402.91		733.76	9
617.31	850.21	91,746.88	6,422.08	8,253.12		733.76	10
611.65	855.87	90,891.01	7,033.73	9,108.99		733.76	11
605.94	861.58	90,029.43	7,639.67	9,970.57		733.76	12
600.20	867.32	89,162.11	8,239.87	10,837.89		733.76	13
594.41	873.11	88,289.00	8,834.28	11,711.00		733.76	14
588.59	878.93	87,410.07	9,422.87	12,589.93		733.76	15
582.73	884.79	86,525.28	10,005.60	13,474.72		733.76	16
576.84	890.68	85,634.60	10,582.44	14,365.40		733.76	17
570.90	896.62	84,737.98	11,153.34	15,262.02		733.76	18
564.92	902.60	83,835.38	11,718.26	16,164.62		733.76	19
558.90	908.62	82,926.76	12,277.16	17,073.24		733.76	20
552.85	914.67	82,012.09	12,830.01	17,987.91		733.76	21
546.75	920.77	81,091.32	13,376.76	18,908.68		733.76	22
540.61	926.91	80,164.41	13,917.37	19,835.59		733.76	23
534.43	933.09	79,231.32	14,451.80	20,768.68		733.76	24
528.21	939.31	78,292.01	14,980.01	21,707.99		733.76	25
521.95	945.57	77,346.44	15,501.96	22,653.56		733.76	26
515.64	951.88	76,394.56	16,017.60	23,605.44		733.76	27
509.30	958.22	75,436.34	16,526.90	24,563.66		733.76	28
502.91	964.61	74,471.73	17,029.81	25,528.27		733.76	29
496.48	971.04	73,500.69	17,526.29	26,499.31		733.76	30

Table 19.4   (Continued)

Interest	Principal	Balance	Accum. Interest	Accum. Principal	Date	Additional Payments	No.
490.00	977.52	72,523.17	18,016.29	27,476.83		733.76	31
483.49	984.03	71,539.14	18,499.78	28,460.86		733.76	32
476.93	990.59	70,548.55	18,976.71	29,451.45		733.76	33
470.32	997.20	69,551.35	19,447.03	30,448.65		733.76	34
463.68	1,003.84	68,547.51	19,910.71	31,452.49		733.76	35
456.98	1,010.54	67,536.97	20,367.69	32,463.03		733.76	36
450.25	1,017.27	66,519.70	20,817.94	33,480.30		733.76	37
443.46	1,024.06	65,495.64	21,261.40	34,504.36		733.76	38
436.64	1,030.88	64,464.76	21,698.04	35,535.24		733.76	39
429.77	1,037.75	63,427.01	22,127.81	36,572.99		733.76	40
422.85	1,044.67	62,382.34	22,550.66	37,617.66		733.76	41
415.88	1,051.64	61,330.70	22,966.54	38,669.30		733.76	42
408.87	1,058.65	60,272.05	23,375.41	39,727.95		733.76	43
401.81	1,065.71	59,206.34	23,777.22	40,793.66		733.76	44
394.71	1,072.81	58,133.53	24,171.93	41,866.47		733.76	45
387.56	1,079.96	57,053.57	24,559.49	42,946.43		733.76	46
380.36	1,087.16	55,966.41	24,939.85	44,033.59		733.76	47
373.11	1,094.41	54,872.00	25,312.96	45,128.00		733.76	48
365.81	1,101.71	53,770.29	25,678.77	46,229.71		733.76	49
358.47	1,109.05	52,661.24	26,037.24	47,338.76		733.76	50
351.07	1,116.45	51,544.79	26,388.31	48,455.21		733.76	51
343.63	1,123.89	50,420.90	26,731.94	49,579.10		733.76	52
336.14	1,131.38	49,289.52	27,068.08	50,710.48		733.76	53
328.60	1,138.92	48,150.60	27,396.68	51,849.40		733.76	54
321.00	1,146.52	47,004.08	27,717.68	52,995.92		733.76	55
313.36	1,154.16	45,849.92	28,031.04	54,150.08		733.76	56
305.67	1,161.85	44,688.07	28,336.71	55,311.93		733.76	57
297.92	1,169.60	43,518.47	28,634.63	56,481.53		733.76	58
290.12	1,177.40	42,341.07	28,924.75	57,658.93		733.76	59
282.27	1,185.25	41,155.82	29,207.02	58,844.18		733.76	60

(Continued)

Table 19.4   (Continued)

Interest	Principal	Balance	Accum. Interest	Accum. Principal	Date	Additional Payments	No.
274.37	1,193.15	39,962.67	29,481.39	60,037.33		733.76	61
266.42	1,201.10	38,761.57	29,747.81	61,238.43		733.76	62
258.41	1,209.11	37,552.46	30,006.22	62,447.54		733.76	63
250.35	1,217.17	36,335.29	30,256.57	63,664.71		733.76	64
242.24	1,225.28	35,110.01	30,498.81	64,889.99		733.76	65
234.07	1,233.45	33,876.56	30,732.88	66,123.44		733.76	66
225.84	1,241.68	32,634.88	30,958.72	67,365.12		733.76	67
217.57	1,249.95	31,384.93	31,176.29	68,615.07		733.76	68
209.23	1,258.29	30,126.64	31,385.52	69,873.36		733.76	69
200.84	1,266.68	28,859.96	31,586.36	71,140.04		733.76	70
192.40	1,275.12	27,584.84	31,778.76	72,415.16		733.76	71
183.90	1,283.62	26,301.22	31,962.66	73,698.78		733.76	72
175.34	1,292.18	25,009.04	32,138.00	74,990.96		733.76	73
166.73	1,300.79	23,708.25	32,304.73	76,291.75		733.76	74
158.06	1,309.46	22,398.79	32,462.79	77,601.21		733.76	75
149.33	1,318.19	21,080.60	32,612.12	78,919.40		733.76	76
140.54	1,326.98	19,753.62	32,752.66	80,246.38		733.76	77
131.69	1,335.83	18,417.79	32,884.35	81,582.21		733.76	78
122.79	1,344.73	17,073.06	33,007.14	82,926.94		733.76	79
113.82	1,353.70	15,719.36	33,120.96	84,280.64		733.76	80
104.80	1,362.72	14,356.64	33,225.76	85,643.36		733.76	81
95.71	1,371.81	12,984.83	33,321.47	87,015.17		733.76	82
86.57	1,380.95	11,603.88	33,408.04	88,396.12		733.76	83
77.36	1,390.16	10,213.72	33,485.40	89,786.28		733.76	84
68.09	1,399.43	8,814.29	33,553.49	91,185.71		733.76	85
58.76	1,408.76	7,405.53	33,612.25	92,594.47		733.76	86
49.37	1,418.15	5,987.38	33,661.62	94,012.62		733.76	87
39.92	1,427.60	4,559.78	33,701.54	95,440.22		733.76	88
30.40	1,437.12	3,122.66	33,731.94	96,877.34		733.76	89
20.82	1,446.70	1,675.96	33,752.76	98,324.04		733.76	90

Table 19.4 (Continued)

Interest	Principal	Balance	Accum. Interest	Accum. Principal	Date	Additional Payments	No.
11.17	1,456.35	219.61	33,763.93	99,780.39		733.76	91
1.46	219.61	0.00	33,765.39	100,000.00		733.76	92

of paying according to the rules. You would still owe over $98,000. If you were forced to sell in a market that had dropped the price of your home by more than a few hundred dollars, how could you make up the difference? Add to that the normal expenses of selling and you could be in trouble. Many people at that time were.

However, had you been working with *The Credit Diet* and been able to double those payments, you'd be in much better shape. As you look at the next chart, you would see that your balance would be only $79,000, or almost $20,000 less than if you had only made one payment per month. If an emergency arose where you'd be forced to sell, you'd at least be able to do it without dipping into your reserves.

However, let's assume that we don't have to go through that again. But even if you're an average American, how much better shape will you be in if you move in seven years? Paying only one payment per month, you'd have a balance of $92,477, or roughly $8,000 less than you originally borrowed. Using the methods that this book suggests would leave you with a balance of only $10,213, or a difference of over $82,000!

You can create a lot of options with $82,000. One of them is to realize that if you stayed put for just eight more months, you'd own the home free and clear. In addition, you'd have to find something to do with the two payments totaling nearly $1,470 every month. Saving those payments in addition to the other savings already in place would go a long way toward achieving financial security.

The catch is that you must be able to double your payments. Following the system you've just read about is the simplest method of working toward that objective. Eliminating other debts can put your financial focus on clearing up the largest debt most people ever encounter. That's why I recommend that this debt be the last one you work on.

Allow yourself a series of victories before launching into the major financial battle of your life. See the rewards from your efforts and let them motivate you to keep going with the last and perhaps largest of all debts. Having lived through a series of successes before tackling this one should provide you with the incentive to keep going. The real benefit is knowing that in addition to eliminating your mortgage, you'll also be filling your other accounts at the same time. Review these mortgage figures in Table 19.4 often as a way to remind yourself how quickly you can progress.

TOOLS THAT YOU CAN USE

Someone once said that if it's worth doing, it's worth writing down. I think that it is extremely important to be able to keep a detailed record of what you're doing. After all, this is your entire financial future at stake. I don't think you want to risk entrusting it to mere memory.

Tracking where your money is going also allows you to make adjustments that are better than wild guesses. For example, if you decide that you want to place more money in your Permanent Wealth account, which accounts would you take the money from? By tracking every deposit, you'll be able to make an educated decision that will not risk your future.

You'll also be able to see when you can move money from your Future Growth account into a better place. Perhaps you were looking at a quality mutual fund that had a minimum starting balance requirement. Tracking how much money was marked for your investments would let you know when you have enough to begin.

You'll also see how quickly you are progressing with this program. That will give you the incentive to continue when things get tough or you begin to question whether or not the program is worth it for you. Being able to see the results of your efforts is important for keeping you driving toward your ultimate destination.

There are several pages of each worksheet so that you can keep records for quite a while. When these run out you can go to your bank and ask for some extra check registers to continue this program. Also, every account has its own affirmation attached to it. Use these words to strengthen you on your way. (See Tables 19.5–19.10, pages 188–207.)

Table 19.5   The Cash Flow Account

All Financial Activity Begins Here

Date	Memo	(+) Interest	(–) Withdrawals	(+) Deposits	Balance

"I am in total control of my financial future."

Table 19.5   The Cash Flow Account

All Financial Activity Begins Here

Date	Memo	(+) Interest	(−) Withdrawals	(+) Deposits	Balance

"I am in total control of my financial future."

Table 19.5   The Cash Flow Account

All Financial Activity Begins Here

Date	Memo	(+) Interest	(−) Withdrawals	(+) Deposits	Balance

"I am in total control of my financial future."

Table 19.5   The Cash Flow Account

All Financial Activity Begins Here

Date	Memo	(+) Interest	(−) Withdrawals	(+) Deposits	Balance

"I am in total control of my financial future."

Table 19.6   The Debt Elimination Account

The Only Account You'll Ever Cancel

Date	Memo	(+) Interest	(−) Withdrawals	(+) Deposits	Balance

"Each withdrawal brings me closer to the freedom I deserve."

Table 19.6   The Debt Elimination Account

The Only Account You'll Ever Cancel

Date	Memo	(+) Interest	(−) Withdrawals	(+) Deposits	Balance

"Each withdrawal brings me closer to the freedom I deserve."

Table 19.6   The Debt Elimination Account

The Only Account You'll Ever Cancel

Date	Memo	(+) Interest	(−) Withdrawals	(+) Deposits	Balance

"Each withdrawal brings me closer to the freedom I deserve."

Table 19.6   The Debt Elimination Account

The Only Account You'll Ever Cancel

Date	Memo	(+) Interest	(−) Withdrawals	(+) Deposits	Balance

"Each withdrawal brings me closer to the freedom I deserve."

Table 19.7   The Future Growth Account

What I Do with Each Deposit Determines My Future

Date	Memo	(+) Interest	(−) Withdrawals	(+) Deposits	Balance

"I plan my future every day because I want to enjoy it when I get there."

Table 19.7   The Future Growth Account

What I Do with Each Deposit Determines My Future

Date	Memo	(+) Interest	(−) Withdrawals	(+) Deposits	Balance

"I plan my future every day because I want to enjoy it when I get there."

Table 19.7   The Future Growth Account

What I Do with Each Deposit Determines My Future

Date	Memo	(+) Interest	(–) Withdrawals	(+) Deposits	Balance

"I plan my future every day because I want to enjoy it when I get there."

Table 19.7   The Future Growth Account

What I Do with Each Deposit Determines My Future

Date	Memo	(+) Interest	(−) Withdrawals	(+) Deposits	Balance

"I plan my future every day because I want to enjoy it when I get there."

Table 19.8   The Permanent Wealth Account

With Each Entry I'm One Step Closer to Freedom

Date	Memo	(+) Interest	(−) Withdrawals	(+) Deposits	Balance

"This is the foundation for my permanent wealth."

Table 19.8   The Permanent Wealth Account

With Each Entry I'm One Step Closer to Freedom

Date	Memo	(+) Interest	(−) Withdrawals	(+) Deposits	Balance

"This is the foundation for my permanent wealth."

Table 19.8   The Permanent Wealth Account

With Each Entry I'm One Step Closer to Freedom

Date	Memo	(+) Interest	(−) Withdrawals	(+) Deposits	Balance

"This is the foundation for my permanent wealth."

Table 19.8   The Permanent Wealth Account

With Each Entry I'm One Step Closer to Freedom

Date	Memo	(+) Interest	(−) Withdrawals	(+) Deposits	Balance

"This is the foundation for my permanent wealth."

Table 19.9   The Totally Fun Account

The Reward for Successful Planning Is Here

Date	Memo	(+) Interest	(−) Withdrawals	(+) Deposits	Balance

"I can enjoy the fruits of my labor guilt-free."

Table 19.9 The Totally Fun Account

The Reward for Successful Planning Is Here

Date	Memo	(+) Interest	(–) Withdrawals	(+) Deposits	Balance

"I can enjoy the fruits of my labor guilt-free."

Table 19.9   The Totally Fun Account

The Reward for Successful Planning Is Here

Date	Memo	(+) Interest	(−) Withdrawals	(+) Deposits	Balance

"I can enjoy the fruits of my labor guilt-free."

Table 19.9   The Totally Fun Account

The Reward for Successful Planning Is Here

Date	Memo	(+) Interest	(−) Withdrawals	(+) Deposits	Balance

"I can enjoy the fruits of my labor guilt-free."

Table 19.10   The Income Security Account

When Money Converts to Finance—You Win

Date	Memo	(+) Interest	(−) Withdrawals	(+) Deposits	Balance

"As soon as enough money is working for me, I'll take plenty of time off."

Table 19.10   The Income Security Account

When Money Converts to Finance—You Win

Date	Memo	(+) Interest	(−) Withdrawals	(+) Deposits	Balance

"As soon as enough money is working for me, I'll take plenty of time off."

Table 19.10   The Income Security Account

When Money Converts to Finance—You Win

Date	Memo	(+) Interest	(−) Withdrawals	(+) Deposits	Balance

"As soon as enough money is working for me, I'll take plenty of time off."

Table 19.10   The Income Security Account

When Money Converts to Finance—You Win

Date	Memo	(+) Interest	(−) Withdrawals	(+) Deposits	Balance

"As soon as enough money is working for me, I'll take plenty of time off."

RESOURCES FOR
THE FUTURE

FIFTEEN MINUTES A DAY

Suppose that before you started this book, I had shared the secret to wealth with you. Imagine that I told you that in order to achieve permanent financial security and freedom, you would need to attend college and earn five degrees. Once you heard that, how long would it take for you to begin giving up on this process?

However, suppose I shared a way for you to acquire that wealth of knowledge without sacrificing your job or time with your family. Interested? It has been said that setting aside just 15 minutes a day to read will result in the equivalent of five college educations in your lifetime. The question is, what do you want to learn? I hope the answer is a variety of things and one of them is your own financial well-being.

One of the things you can do to develop comfort and familiarity with finance as you take this journey is to expand your horizons. Read books that can help you get a better grasp on how to get the most out of your money. That way, when you finally are free from debt, you can plan your financial future with confidence.

There are many books out there with claims of surefire success if you follow the patterns described on their pages. By reading them as you build yourself a secure future, you'll be in a better position to decide what will work for you when the time comes to move your money around.

WHAT I'VE READ

Think and Grow Rich, Napoleon Hill—Ballantine Books Edition, 1983. This is the granddaddy of them all. I have followed the principles in this book in every aspect of my life. Hill believes, as do I, that any great accomplishment must be preceded by an equal thought. Preparing yourself mentally before the money arrives is the greatest way to insure that it stays in your possession until you decide what to do with it.

The Wealthy Barber, David Chilton—Prima Publishing, 1998. Using a fictional barber to share his advice, Chilton helps the reader understand the "get rich slowly" concept of asset allocation. It's an easy story to follow and you'll find yourself substituting your life for those of the characters. The advice from the barber is simple and to the point. Most important, you can see the possibilities of great results in the future.

Anything by Suze Orman. I believe her greatest strength as an author with financial expertise is her balance. Money, while important, is never allowed to take top priority and therefore control one's life. Her practices for money management reflect her life values, which I believe is key to sustaining one's financial soundness.

Rich Dad, Poor Dad, Robert Kiyosaki with Sharon L. Lechter, CPA—1998. Stressing the importance of money knowledge before money acquisition, Kiyosaki shares his experiences of growing up with an educated father who wasn't wise in the ways of finance. His friend's father teaches him how to use money as a tool through working examples and easy-to-understand lessons.

The Pig and the Python, David Cork with Susan Lightstone—Prima Publishing, 1998. What causes money to do what it does? Cork and Lightstone share the effects that aging baby boomers have on virtually every aspect of society and finance. They offer educated opinions on why certain things happened and how you might be able to take advantage of future opportunities as the boomer generation ages.

There are many other books out there, and each will offer a different perspective on how to get the most from your money. I recommend reading as many as possible to see the different ideas that are explained. The more information you can digest, the easier it will be to make financial decisions when the time comes.

While it's not essential to understand every nuance and definition in the financial arena, it will be important to be familiar with as many terms as possible. This way you won't be intimidated when getting advice. You'll also feel better about not taking certain pieces of advice when they don't suit you.

Another source of reading material is a daily paper called *Investor's Business Daily*. It may intimidate you the first time you buy one. That's okay. Buy it anyway. Begin by reading nothing but the headlines. Get familiar with certain words that seem to appear often. Then pick a story or two each day and try to understand what the information could mean to a potential investor like you.

It won't be long before you can understand a good portion of the terminology, and you may even feel comfortable with it. It's also a great guide to follow stocks, bonds, and mutual funds on a daily basis. As I mentioned earlier in the book, why not pretend to invest money in areas you feel comfortable with and track it through this paper? See how you do before you use any of your real money.

POSITIVE CHANGES

Reading, studying, getting comfortable—these are all things that will allow you to stay in control of your finances. Obtaining information and understanding that info will eliminate needless worry about money in your life. I think we can agree that better decisions are always made when there is a lack of stress or pressure to make them. When you sit back and evaluate all of the facts without a deadline or past due notice hanging over your head, clearer thoughts prevail.

Rather than constantly worrying about where the next dollar might come from, you spend time analyzing the best place to put your earnings. There's more comfort in planning the best places to put your money than in scheming what to say when a bill collector calls.

As I mentioned earlier in this book, as well as in many of my speaking programs, great results are always preceded by great thoughts. When your thoughts are constantly under pressure to solve the problem of paying bills, your results are often just that—solutions for today only. However, by reading informative books like those I've mentioned, your mind begins to become prepared for a future that you've planned rather than one that seems to sneak up on you and create stressful emergencies.

MATERIALISM VERSUS CAPITALISM

When you begin using this system, some of your friends might call you materialistic. You may be accused of spending too much time thinking about money and not enough time thinking of them. Jealousy aside, are they going to help with your bills? Will they come up with money to put your kids through college or fund your retirement?

What do you think they'd do if you told them that they were actually more materialistic than you'll ever be? They'd laugh at first, then ask how you could possibly say that.

To me, the definition of *materialism* is a nearly constant concern for money. Where will it come from? How much do I need? When will I be able to get ahead? And so on. Capitalism is the acquisition of money in exchange for the delivery of goods and services. Capitalists use the free enterprise system to develop new markets and products for those markets in an effort to make a profit. Many millionaires have come from the practice of free enterprise.

As a speaker, I've had occasion to be hired by many millionaires to speak at their events. While I was writing this book, I was able to discuss my thoughts and ideas with them. Interestingly, I was the one who had to bring money up in order to discuss it. It seemed that the last thing they ever wanted to talk about was how much they had or how much they were making.

In other words, those who thought about or focused on money the most were generally the ones who didn't have any. The thought of money and of how to get more was constantly taking up the space in their minds. That's true materialism.

While I've painted with a broad brush in the above example, I think I can conclude one thing about people and money. After seeing and living both sides of the issue, I've determined that in addition to everything else that money does, it also magnifies. That's right. Money magnifies. Whatever you were before you achieved any wealth will only become larger as your fortune grows. If you have a tendency to be a bit humble, money will make you more so. If you're charitable, you'll contribute more. And if you have been a jerk, money will only serve to make you an even bigger one.

The time to learn to manage yourself as well as your money is while you're acquiring it. Determine who you'd like to be once you've reached your goal, and then begin taking the steps to insure that you arrive at both objectives at the same time. Only then will all of the effort you've put forth have any real value.

AFTERWORD

Since I began sharing this information with others, one question seems to come up more often than others: How do you determine how much money to put into each account? I'd love nothing more than to give you a concrete answer to solve your dilemma, but the fact is, it really doesn't matter.

Stop putting so much pressure on yourself and thereby delaying your start toward the freedom you deserve. Many of you had fun buying the things you did to get into debt. Let your journey into financial security be at least as much fun. Any money going toward your freedom is exactly the right amount.

For those of you who really do need a concrete answer complete with a formula before you get going, I'll give you the one I used. I want you to understand that this formula was developed after the fact. What I mean is, after I was doing it for a while, I simply calculated the percentages I was using and kept it as a record. If these formulas worked for me, looking backward, I'm certain you can use them going forward.

The formula is geared toward getting free.

1. With the exception of your mortgage, add all your monthly payments together.
2. Take the total and divide it into your gross income (total of payments/gross income = debt ratio)

Example

You earn $2000. You pay $800 in monthly payments. $800 ÷ $2000 = .40 or 40%. Your debt ratio is 40 percent.

The percentage of income owed to debt should be the percentage paid into the Debt Elimination account. The other accounts can be set up as you see fit.

Example

Assume a 40 percent debt ratio.

Permanent Wealth Account	10%
Totally Fun Account	20%
Debt Elimination Account	40%
Income Security Account	20%
Future Growth Account	10%

You can use this formula if you feel more comfortable with structure, or you can mix and match as determined by your personal goals. If you feel that your number one objective is to be able to retire once you're debt-free, you may want to put more into your Permanent Wealth, Future Growth, and Income Security accounts. While this will lengthen the time it takes to eliminate all of your debts, you'll also be in a much better financial position to retire securely once you're there.

The two most important things for you to realize about this book are that, first and foremost, you can do this—it's simple and requires only a small amount of commitment to achieve the desired results—and second, as soon as you take the first step, you place yourself and your future ahead of 95 percent of the rest of the population. You are in control of your future. From the moment you complete this book and make your first financial move, you are in control of your life. For some of you this may be a new feeling. That's okay. Enjoy it! This is only the beginning.

INDEX

ABOUT THE AUTHOR

John Fuhrman is an award-winning member of the National Speakers Association. He's been selected as an Honored Professional in the *National Register's Who's Who in Executives and Professionals*. His books have sold around the world and he has spoken across the continent.

His articles have appeared in countless magazines and he has been interviewed on over 300 radio and television stations. He is considered to be one of the top "activational" speakers in America. Rather than just motivating, he gets the audience to take the action needed to change their lives.

If your company would be interested in John's Debt Reduction Programs, or if you have a group of people that may be interested, contact the office of Frame of Mind, Inc. at (888) 883-3303, toll-free. You can also e-mail any comments to John through his web site at www.CreditDiet.com.

Please feel free to send us your success stories. You can mail them to Credit Diet, 89 Bayberry Lane, Manchester, NH 03104.

Watch for the following upcoming *Credit Diet* releases: *The Credit Diet for Kids* and *The Credit Diet for College Students*.